Roots, Shoots & Wings

***

Bette Moffett

SHIRES PRESS

4869 Main Street
P.O. Box 2200
Manchester Center, VT 05255
www.northshire.com/printondemand.php

Roots, Shoots & Wings
©2010 Bette Moffett
All rights reserved

ISBN Number: 978-1-60571-077-8
Library of Congress Number: 2010911647

NORTHSHIRE BOOKSTORE

Building Community, One Book at a Time
This book was printed at the Northshire Bookstore, a family-owned, independent bookstore in Manchester Ctr., Vermont, since 1976. We are committed to excellence in bookselling. The Northshire Bookstore's mission is to serve as a resource for information, ideas, and entertainment while honoring the needs of customers, staff, and community.

Printed in the United States of America

To my children, grandchildren and great grandchildren, who are living their own stories. They give me hope.

Homage to Memory

If any one faculty of our nature may be called more wonderful than the rest, I do think it is memory. There seems something more speakingly incomprehensible in the powers, the failures, the inequalities of memory, than in any other of our intelligence's. The memory is sometimes so retentive, so serviceable, so obedient; at others, again, so tyrannical, so beyond control! We are to be sure a miracle every way; but our powers of recollecting and of forgetting do seem peculiarly past finding out.
— Jane Austen, Mansfield Park

"I will tell you something about stories. They aren't just entertainment. Don't be fooled. They are all we have, you see...You don't have anything if you don't have stories..."
— Leslie Marmon Silko, from Marianne Lust's 2009 MARROWBONE.

Anais Nin said, *"We write to taste life twice."*

"Anybody who has survived his childhood has enough information about life to last the rest of his days."
— Flannery O'Connor

Springtime in Plymouth County, Iowa

Lula Miller Little cranked the family Model A into motion early Monday morning, May 27, 1924, and drove to keep her prenatal appointment with Dr. Raw, in Pierson, six miles south of the farm.

After a thirty-step climb to his office, Dr. Raw examined her and announced, "You're due—I'll see you at your house."

As she reached the street, Dr. Raw leaned out his window and yelled down, "Don't you crank that car or you'll deliver on the curb." Bill Blevin, a passerby, got her back on the road.

Emma, the hired girl, made up my parents' double brass bed to receive me. Dad was close by and useful—Mother spoke of the strength of his hands and the support of the sturdy brass headboard sustaining her through my brother Joe's birth until Dr. Raw arrived by horse and carriage in 1922. A midwife coaxed my father, John Bammer Little, into being at the same address in 1899.

Outside, on my birthday, old fashioned yellow rose blooms crowded the east bedroom windows—just as the Drama Class students from Kingsley High School did 15 years later on a sympathy visit when I had the mumps. Swollen glands were one thing, but giving up the lead role of *The Duchess Bounces In*, was also crushing.

Prairie Provenance

    I came from the prairie—space, fresh air, big sky, jagged lightning, all of which have given me an innate sense of boundless freedom and spirit.

    Any attitude of contribution—a giving back, came from my family and community. Good neighboring was hard work as you agreed to always be there and it could mean pulling a shredded arm out of a corn sheller, removing an inhaled barley beard from a hay stacker's throat, or pulling a colt from a troubled mare.

    I observed these scenes with gravity and resignation. Resilience and challenge were marked traits in my home. I heard a Federal Agricultural Agent in the 1930's tell my Father he would have to slaughter all new pigs to control the pork price; the same summer, encephalitis wiped out our twenty-two horses. The following year, the seed was prepared, crops were planted, spring unfolded innocent of the past. Onward and upward—that's my heritage!

    I came home without ever having left; you take your childhood with you.

Humble Housing

We all lived in leaky clapboard houses; insulation might have been old newspapers, stuffed in the walls like an inadvertent archive. Windows rattled with the elements—floors downstairs did have carpets, linoleum in the kitchen and pantry area. Register grates let warm air from the dining room heater upstairs. Bricks were heated in the woodstove oven nightly, wrapped in newspapers and promptly delivered to beds upstairs. Winter mornings, it wasn't unusual for the bed quilts to be covered with snow blown in from a storm. Dressing in winter was a race to the space behind the kitchen woodstove. Joe usually beat me to it.

Dinner parties were held in our dining room, which sometimes received feathers from our pillow fights. They drifted down upon bridge tables below. After the first landing, laughter rose and we receded.

There was a brick house that we passed on the way to town. I always fantasized about how tight, elegant and warm a home it must be.

Electrification and Illumination

We had a Delco Electric unit placed just inside the barnyard gate, which provided nighttime illumination to all of the outbuildings. Also, it connected the household to the world through the RCA radio in the parlor, complete with a Morning Glory Speaker Horn, as well as the smaller Bakelite radio in the kitchen.

Candles and kerosene lamps were only used upstairs. The bright mantle-style gas lamp flooded the evening kitchen space most, especially the round oak table which doubled as the dining, homework and reading area for everyone.

Dreamtime

I had lots of time as a child. Much of it evolved while rolling about in the tall bluegrass—a buffer between our house and the road. I remember the sounds of buzzing insects and the smell of the earth. I was consumed with the idea that we all saw colors and objects differently. Just like we had individual filters to peer through. I thought about it all the time.

When I was seven I read constantly and kept a notebook of what I thought were beautifully written phrases, sentences and certain words. How I would love to see that collection again. Words that appealed gained entrance into our daily exchange, much, I'm sure, to the family's amusement. My best friend was the daily blank page in my diary that recorded my innocence, pure thought, unabashed blurting which seemed so important then. It was a loyal non-judgmental ally willing to learn more about my cosmic curiosity.

Willow Whistles

A rite of spring was walking through our feed lot south of the big lawn with my Father into the willow grove.

He would cut off about six limber willow branches one inch through and begin to tap the exterior skin with his silver pen knife, until the jacket was loose enough to slide back and forth on the slippery core.

Then he would carefully make a cut in the bark—not deep, but essentially just right to permit the airflow through the beveled groove. He blew his first note. It was always trial and error before I could make the sound he did, but I would adjust the bright green outer skin hole until I succeeded. It was the second highest thrill to learning how to stretch a roadside grass blade from my index finger, anchored by my thumb and blow along the edge creating an unearthly screech.

Grand Parents

Nestled into a residential block of Pierson, Iowa, was a small compact brick house, the home of Lina and Henri de Lambert, my great grandparents. We would visit them every Saturday and as a child I knew there was something different about them. They were French and cooked with garlic (onion was the wildest flavor in my home), and Grandma Lina planted an exquisite herb garden with bricked paths forming and containing a knot design in her front yard—a child's dream path. She baked all day Friday and filled at least six pantry shelves with rich pastries. Joe and I would rehearse the choices all week long. He favored a dark chocolate cake, and I, a flaky pastry wrapped around dark chocolate. A glass of milk and manners at the table followed. Mother was a very special granddaughter to them. Grandmother Lina always packed a basketful of treats to carry us through the weekend.

Our Grandmother Mae Miller lived on a dirt road near Lawton, Iowa. She was a very hearty, generous woman who always let me play in her attic which was full of many relics from the past. A huge trunk bulged with turn-of-the-century clothing. My favorite items were the women's large brimmed hats, trimmed with colorful ostrich feathers, fancy shoes, beaded reticules, long gloves and one parasol. Who wore this finery? Not sensible Grandmother Miller. Her life was too sober as a mother of five children and wife to a not-too-dependable husband, my gambling Grandfather, Ed Miller. She was a good scratch cook and took each day calmly. One visit, Mother misread the rain clouds and the Model A fairly danced down the greasy dirt road whose ruts had filled with water concealing their depth. No amusement park could have created a more challenging ride. Drenched and drained, we reached our gravel road and marveled at how the cloudburst had missed our farm.

Grandmother Elizabeth Bammer Little, mother of seven, lived in Kingsley. Grandfather John William Little died before my birth. Mother was promised $1,000 by him if she would bear a red-haired daughter with blue eyes. She got it half right, but my eyes were hazel.

Good Neighbors

Joe, 14 years old, was very enterprising. Weekly, for four years, he delivered *The Country Gentleman*, *The Delineator*, and *The Saturday Evening Post* magazines to 25 houses on our four-mile gravel road east of Kingsley. The weight of his packed, cloth bag caused his right shoulder to drop noticeably. During high school he experienced quite a growth spurt, which landed him in shoulder braces to guide his posture. A football injury added a shoulder blade cast.

Extreme winter conditions challenged his delivery schedule, and the thought of all that mail piling up at the post office threatened his perfect record. Soon, he was wrestling odd pieces of wood accumulated on the back porch for repair use. Into the kitchen came his long Flexible Flier sled. Then, the rough looking box was joined to the sled.

At supper he announced that he was walking the icy road to Kingsley the next morning to check on Grandmother Little, pick up and pack all the neighbor's mail in delivery sequence. And he did, though not without frostbite and occasional cave-ins—which kept tipping the cargo. The neighbors' disbelief and joy kept him going, as did warm fires and food along the way. This early glimpse of his goodness was prophetic.

The next measurable treat for the snowbound was the sound of the plow from town. When our three-week winter vacation was over, Dad would ride Rowdy to the one-room schoolhouse on Sunday afternoon and build a fire in the central heater so that Miss Diller and her twelve students could reunite in comfort.

Monday was spent telling and listening to snow and family stories. King of the Mountain and Fox and Geese were the obvious recess games. We managed to build and pack a white mountain way over our heads—dig out steps for climbing; then slipping and sliding swiftly to the bottom, tirelessly. Soaked outer garments were draped all over the school seats and desks for the rest of the day, creating the aroma of wet chicken feathers from wet wool. All part of the winter games.

The One-Room School

Garfield No.5 was located on an acre of prairie untouched by a plow. Joe and I walked a quarter mile east and one mile north to and from school every day. Eleven other students had the same distance to cover, more or less. School hours were 8 a.m. to 4 p.m. I arrived on time, but mapped the ditches on the trip home to locate wild strawberry plants, buttercups, straw flowers, violets, Queen Anne's lace, hawkweed, chicory, pink clover, rabbit's foot clover, Sweet William, and the state flower, the wild rose. I tried to transplant wild flowers in a bed near our house—but watering was a problem. I was aware of every patch of prairie beauty along the path.

The school day started with the hope of being chosen by Miss Diller to run the flag up our pole. Then we gathered around and pledged allegiance in unison. Desks were anchored to the floor with two-by-fours and arranged in two long rows in front of Miss Diller's desk, which was on a raised platform. Six blackboards bordered by the alphabet in script—upper case and lower—filled the back wall. Also on the platform rested the seat of learning—the recitation bench.

Classes, one through six, were called up to recite daily. It was an excellent review if you had time to listen. I loved hearing my brother's lessons, which were two years ahead of me. Some nights I would try to remember and help him with his homework. We worked at the round oak kitchen table, and Miss Diller, who boarded in our home, was upstairs in her room with her own homework.

Dad was Chairman of the school board. I remember discussions with Mother and Miss Diller about the Wright boy, Wilbur. Iowa was proud of their literacy goals and passed a law requiring that all students must master their grade level subjects or repeat the year. Wilbur Wright was 22 years old and was clearly becoming a menace and a repeater.

One afternoon, he left his seat and walked about the room systematically pulling down all the window shades. Then, displaying unimaginable strength, he proceeded to pick up each row of seats (with the students in them) and drop them abruptly. The room was tense. I watched as Joe rose and tapped Billy Hardie and Russell Hiller on the shoulder. The three of them grabbed Wilbur and, with main strength and awkwardness, removed him.

Miss Diller was in tears, the rest of us were praying, I think, while the schoolboy struggle ensued in the yard. I was sure they were doing terrible damage to each other—but no sound reached us. I don't remember breathing. Eventually, the door swung wide and hit the opposite wall. Still paralyzed, we watched Joe take his seat, then Billy entered and finally Russell—all spent and very roughed up.

Miss Diller choked, "Where's Wilbur?" The three numbly pointed in the direction of the open door. Uninvited and unannounced the school emptied with Miss Diller bringing up the rear. The boys had managed to tie Wilbur to the flagpole. He had been through a battle, that was clear.

Something had to be done and this called on Dad's peacemaking skills. Suddenly, Wilbur was needed on his family farm. Discipline had never been a problem up until then. Language was. Miss Diller had a virtual kind of United Nations to decipher and unite. The students were German, Swedish, French and American. It was a comical charade at times. They were all good neighbors and willing to learn.

Miss Diller asked Mother if she could invite the school to spend an evening making and pulling taffy. We had great time enjoying a universal treat; candy. Another night, it was popcorn balls, and we learned three different languages in the process.

Miss Diller's Beau

My parents always insisted that our five boarders use the parlor to entertain their friends. Miss Diller, our teacher, was the only taker, albeit seldom. Wyndam Bauer was her bashful beau. One night, Joe and I snuck behind the couch while Miss Diller played some dreary selection on the piano. We could see Wyndam's feet in the doorway. I peeked around the corner and saw a yellow rectangle held behind his back. I later realized it was a box of Whitman chocolates. He moved to the couch and sat down. Joe and I were crowded flat against the wall and breathing hard. Could he hear us? Miss Diller kept playing. We were stuck but took turns motioning to each other to leave. Joe slithered to the doorway opening, which opened into the hall, first. I soon followed him out the front door. We just sat down in the grass and leaned against a tree laughing at our dull adventure.

Daily Pleasure

As a child, four or five years old, I remember the security of being with our household at meal time. Every night after supper, the last of the dessert was portioned out and scraped clean off the plate. Dad would still be conversing with the hired men about tomorrow's planting plans, haying, spraying fruit trees, depending on the season. He would push back his chair at the end of the round oak table closest to the wood stove reservoir and reach for an ashtray, which was always resting on the nickel bumper. He rose to select wooden matches from a tin dispenser on the wall close to the south kitchen window. On his left hand he wore his Masonic ring, an elaborately designed gold band burnished by daily chores and specifically the habit of striking the red phosphorous match head on the Masonic emblem design. The blue flame that rose from his left fist resting on the table mesmerized me. His timing was crisp. As the flame reached its most beautiful stage, he brought forth a spanking white Chesterfield cigarette from his shirt pocket, placed it in his mouth, dragged deeply, creating a toasted aroma, which I loved — a wisp of smoke curling over his head. Our hired men rolled their own with one hand on horseback and two hands on land.

A Moving Target

Joe received a 410 rifle when he was nine years old, as did most boys that age. They hunted with their fathers and uncles, and I can remember Dad drilling Joe on the care and cleaning of his gun.

Joe also had a BB gun, and was so keen to improve his aim that he decided he needed a moving target to better approximate hunting conditions. That would be me, wearing Dad's heavy canvas duck coat, running back and forth between the clothesline posts. It never occurred to us that this might be risky.

Joe was a good shot and got better. When Mother needed pigeons for a pigeon and biscuit pie, Joe would fire-off six shots and enter the kitchen with six birds.

Events Beyond My Farm

1924. Edward VIII, the Prince of Wales, a forty-year-old restless bachelor, abdicated the British Throne so that he could marry Wallis Simpson, a commoner.

Civil War raged in Spain.

Kafka, the Czech writer who noted that "a book is an eye upon the frozen sea within us," died.

Ghandi spoke about the future of India.

Calvin Coolidge was President of the Untied States.

1934. Queen Mary of England christened the ocean liner *Queen Mary*.

School Chores

Fresh water for drinking and washing had to be carried to the school, daily. Miss Diller would assign a pair of students every morning and place a carved wooden yoke with leather pads on our shoulders. A couple of wooden buckets swung at our sides.

Of course, we weren't always the same height, which made the quarter mile run downhill to the Rock's home rather clumsy. Mrs. Rock had her pump already primed for our needs. Chattering in German she patted our heads as if to give us strength for the hill climb ahead. Buckets were full and time to take off—evenly, if possible. Sometimes we both got a shoe-full. Laughter was the worst—it destroyed our rhythm. We were always a welcome sight on the school porch. I also recall that we would practice our spelling words to make the time and task pass quicker.

Two trophies were awarded every Friday: one for the perfect speller and the other for penmanship; two important skills for life. At the end of our 6th grade year, we were given a comprehensive test to qualify for the Kingsley Town School, four miles west.

A somber Miss Christine Peterson with a golden braid appeared and administered the test. She walked up and down the inside and outside aisles of our classroom, exuding all her authority as Superintendent of Schools. We passed and then worried about the next step, facing a consolidated collection of strangers at the Town School. Joe was a sophomore and liked it, especially basketball, baseball, and football. All students who were needed for farm chores were given permission to drive to and from, which Joe did sometimes. One car was pretty hard for a family to share. Girls didn't drive.

Teacher Admiration

From five years of age to twelve, I only had two schoolteachers, Miss Diller and Miss Beck, and both young women lived with my family during the academic year. I always wondered how their lives equipped them to know so much. I'm sure their interviews and job descriptions must have paled beside the actual challenges on the job.

Managing a confluence of languages, for instance. English was spoken in some homes, not all. The homework got done, though I remember papers worn thin and ripped from the erasure of too many errors. Reading was taught phonetically; those new sounds were like attempting another language. We all learned together through repetition. We read aloud daily at our grade levels. Remember, we had that hidden weapon, that guaranteed rote and retention; the recitation bench. Each class rotated throughout the day, regurgitating math, spelling, grammar, art, history, poetry, music and geography complete with pulled down maps which provided an excellent review and a look ahead. Willing students paced themselves. Extra help was offered and given before and after school—even recess. I liked to try to take dictation when I learned to write script but was soon left behind. We were constantly prompted by that beneficial bench.

Measles, chicken pox, scarletina, mumps or hard colds never seemed to visit the teachers. We never had a substitute. Emergencies, maintaining the central heater fires, playground mishaps, bee stings seemed to be handled with confidence, calm and old fashioned common sense and remedies. Diplomacy was modeled when differences arose.

Physical Education was vigorously practiced, daily. The four-mile walk to and from school was not enough. New games were frequently introduced. Music was a favorite subject. The self-winding Victrola had many cylinders for choice.

All students took part in our Minstrel Shows. Patriotic songs and hymns were sung around the teacher at the keyboard. Regardless of talent, music prevailed rhythmically and lyrically. Choral Reading, a novel idea which we all loved, was presented to our families and the Superintendent, Mrs. Christine Peterson. It resembled the Gospel call and response pattern or a Modern Greek Chorus. We performed at the drop of a national holiday, birthday or season. One selection, which we called "Hospo-de-powno-wee", and which could have been in Latin or Russian, was chanted with great spirit.

We declaimed! Much poetry and prose were committed to memory at all levels. We were coached on delivery until we all knew each other's lines. Eye contact, no distracting body movement was emphasized.

My father, who had attended the same school, could recite all of my selections then and later into his life.

A Kitchen Concert

I don't know how old I was when I first heard my Father sing, *When You Wear a Little White Gardenia*, but after the first time, it happened a lot.

As he busily propped a silver hand mirror in the south kitchen window, he hummed the tune and then pressed the straight edge razor blade back and forth on the strop that hung in the wainscotted corner. Next, he vigorously stirred his brush in the shaving mug and lathered his face—now singing with much expression.

Dad had a nice tenor voice with which he rhythmically phrased the song lyrics with his razor strokes—coming out even with the finishing gesture of the hot towel treatment. I loved this ritual because it was a tender special time of just being with my father. He would pat my head or wink when he left his task and then I would ready myself for the walk to school.

Ironing Apprentice

Throughout the year, Monday was wash day, and Tuesday was devoted to ironing. Climate was cruel to bare hands when clothes were hung out in the winter. Bringing in the frozen shapes created a cat's cradle line design in the kitchen behind the wood stove until they reached the perfect dampness for ironing.

Summertime was a joy, except for the heat from the wood stove and the sad irons. If clothes dried out too much, Mother would put the sprinkling cap on a full catsup bottle of water and anointed every layer of fabric and then rolled it up, sailor style, and tucked it into the refrigerator door pocket. When the sad irons were just right to her moistened index finger, Mother made the most of her chores by turning on one of her favorite radio programs—the Literary Classics. While Orson Wells read from *Citizen Kane*, she listened and dreamed. Finished shirts were hung on hangers. When completely dry she carefully folded them and buttoned the placket so they fit perfectly in the shirt bureau drawer. One day, Tolstoy's *Anna Karenina* was being read and Mother was crying and sobbing so hard that I got caught-up in the love story too. I borrowed the book from our library so we could cry together again about those Russian heartaches. I remember another hot summer day that brought us to tears; when France fell to the Germans in World War II.

I wanted to iron like my Mother. I asked if I could iron Joe's white shirts. She suggested that I start on the hired men's blue chambray shirts first to see how I got along. I wasn't too sure about how to judge the heat of the sad irons because scorching was to be avoided so we talked a lot about choosing irons from the cooler part of the stovetop for certain parts of the shirt, like the collar, cuffs and the placket. Out of the refrigerator she grabbed a rolled-up blue wad and shook it out vigorously, spreading it over the board with her hands. The lesson was starting. I was only going to watch.

First, iron the collar on the wrong side, then the right, making sure there were no wrinkles. On to the cuffs, wrong side first then the right, again checking to see there were no wrinkles. Next the shoulder yoke and then the placket front and back. Lastly, touch up the collar and cuffs so they are a smooth, slick plane. Button the placket and place the shirt on a hanger until completely dry.

Eventually, I graduated to Joe's and Dad's white shirts—but not without learning about what to do about scorching.

Three Reflections

When I was eight, three personalities filled my star-struck imagination. Two came to visit.

The first, Aunt Erma, arrived one summer day. She drove her red lacquer convertible into our house yard and looked like a movie star. She wore a blinding white linen tailored dress accessorized by a red snakeskin belt, matching over the shoulder bag, and completed with red snakeskin sling back platform shoes, flaming red lipstick and perfect matching nails.

She was full of life and talk of adventure and was so glamorous! During a snack of lemonade and dream bars she showed me a map of Cuba—all marked to indicate the roads she traveled in a rented Chevrolet. Aunt Erma was an Accessory Buyer for a prominent Chicago store and she favored the Cuban markets because they were so different, very flamboyant, offering exquisite fabric prints, jewelry, and belts for less money than other wholesale markets.

I couldn't imagine being paid to select beautiful products to sell. I never saw enough of her, as her job demanded a lot of travel time to find new markets for her customers. The seed had been planted; my sights were refocused.

Radio was our lifeline. Livestock reports often mentioned my father's quality beef/pork shipments. Then there was the Fred Waring Gleeclub and Wayne King's saxophone-smooth orchestra rendering the lasting standards of the 30's. News, domestic and international, as well as the daily *Sioux City Journal* newspaper, were full partners at supper.

And that's how I met Haile Selassie, who was thrust upon the scene during World War II, when Italy invaded Ethiopia. When I inquired about the whereabouts of the country, Dad said, "Get the globe and try to find it." I did. Ethiopia was pink and Haile Selassie was the ruler of this country. *Pathé News* featured many clips about him and he was a small figure who appeared to be about my size, wearing lavish golden sashes and bejeweled tunics. Later, I learned what a tyrant he was and that ended the infatuation.

Then there was J.D. Miller, who showed up one warm fall afternoon. What a treat he was. Mother hugged him and cried as if she were embracing a brother. He was a distant nephew. J.D. was disowned by his famous surgeon father in Chicago because instead of attending college, he chose the life of the artist and traveled all over Europe. My family only had sketchy news of the whole story, but Mother always supported him and wanted him to stay.

He was dressed in velvety suedes, colors found in a New England autumn, a Rembrandt tam and a silk scarf at his throat. His backpack was seasoned and scuffed. Would he show me what he carried? We went into the parlor and spread out on the sofa all of his pencils, brushes and watercolor paper blocks. A painting of Austria was on top. His handmade taupe suede shoes were so beautiful. I couldn't help thinking about all the foreign soil they had trod.

We kept him talking until suppertime and then in to the night. It was a very exciting visit for all of us.

I showed him to his bedroom upstairs and gave him my candle to use for a light. I wanted to write in his handsome leather bound journal. I couldn't sleep just thinking about his stories one wall away. Would I ever cross borders into another land? J.D. started me onto a dream and another path to follow some day.

Close to the Stars

Woody Allen didn't know me personally, but he told my passionate story in his movie, *The Purple Rose of Cairo*.

When Mother went to the Beauty Shop I always waited and read *Photoplay*, the Hollywood movie magazine which featured pages of sepia and color photos of all the stars.

Our Deluxe Theatre charged 10¢ admission and nothing if you wanted to see the film twice. Sometimes Mr. Thomas, the owner, would give me advertising posters, which were the last glimpse on my bedroom wall and the first glance in the morning.

The stars distractions and music, which I listened to all night on my radio, was my special dreamtime.

Show Biz

I remember the acrid smell of burning cork in our kitchen at that time. When it cooled, Dad would cup my chin with his big hand as he straddled a kitchen chair. The other hand held the black cork that he applied to my eager, tilted face. I was probably eight, and in my third Minstrel Show at Garfield No. 5.

The other classmates underwent similar transformations in their homes. Then, we'd all pull on bib overalls, bright blouses, red polka dot kerchiefs, and socks—no shoes were worn.

We did a lot of singing in our school and this night we sang slave songs, sometimes in harmony. Families provided a very lively audience and seemed to enjoy our programs. No cultural history explanation or discussion was ever offered in school or at home. A missed opportunity.

1932 Mail

Daily mail kept hope alive on the farm. Simon Gable was our carrier on the four-mile Rural Free Delivery route east of Kingsley. He was the link to miles beyond our farm via the *Sioux City Journal* newspaper. He arrived promptly at eleven o'clock a.m. He knew everything: who was home, who wasn't, which cars in the yard meant visitors, who owned the runaway horse on Cross Hill, and who wrote the most letters and received the most mail—that was Joe.

Besides his weekly load of *Colliers, Country Gentlemen, Saturday Evening Posts* and *Delineators* for his route, Joe received various requested samples of new and old products. Somehow Simon found room in our huge metal mailbox, on which Dad had lettered his name with black paint on one side. Dad mowed a path from our front porch through the tall bluegrass to the gate that rested atop the ditch full of weaving hollyhocks, rooted near the mailbox post and the uneven edge of gravel road. The path was duly shoveled during winter.

My mail jealousy was leavened by offering to clip coupons in the undelivered magazines. I fancied myself as his secretary and labeled my bedroom door as such. Seated at an oak desk I had made for my 4-H project, I made lists of our inventory for our Sunday Country Store in the parlor. We had four orange crates which, when pushed together, formed our countertop. Inside were items for sale. A cigar box served as our bank.

After church, friends and relatives would come by to visit and often buy gloves, belts, pencils, fountain pens, soap, hairnets, glue, jewelry, ozite pads, 8oz. Mr. Goodbars, Babe Ruth, Clark, Hershey and Mounds candy bars, combs, mirrors and whatever else arrived in the mail. I had a tin cash register that worked some times, but I loved adding up every sale. Sunday evenings, after we popped a dishpan full of popcorn for everyone, we counted the money and Joe plotted his next steps.

  Another endeavor of his concerned trapping gophers. I was excited to be a part of this, too, and taught how to sight gopher mounds in our two pastures, how to dig and find the crossroads, and how to deftly place the trap without springing it. Since badger, fox and gopher holes were leg breakers for our grazing livestock, we kept busy. Joe was paid a bounty by the state for gopher paws, which he cured in cigar boxes of salt stacked on the top shelf of his closet. Underneath, on the floor, rested his high-top leather Redwing lace-up brown boots, which I coveted and tried on, wishing they were mine. Back to sandals.

Suddenly the Stranger

I'd just celebrated my ninth birthday—a fourth grader now enjoying her new pair of sandals while meandering along the quarter mile stretch of road to our mailbox. I was so happy, carrying my new pencils and skipping on the hard track in the middle of the road. I could see our orchard with the windmill, my house and the farm buildings. Suddenly, I heard a noise, an odd jingly noise like fancy horses have on their harnesses sometimes. It was behind me, coming from the east. I turned and saw a tall woman wrapped in so many colors, in a loose blouse and long layered skirts—combinations of style and pattern I had never seen. I stared too long as she fixed on me and moved nearer.

Quickening my step, but not running, I reached the edge of our orchard and felt secure. Then, a large rough hand slipped over mine. I never looked up. My chest hurt—I couldn't catch my breath—and I remember walking straight ahead and fast. She said, "Where do you live?" Could she feel the tension in my hand? Did she know? Head down, I glanced at the wild roses across from my beloved hollyhock garden caressing the J.B. Little mailbox. Again, she asked, 'Where do you live?" I picked up my gait, wondering how this terror would end.

We had now passed through the gate—the big wooden gate with my father's name printed on the metal sign from The Progressive Farmer's Organization—into our barnyard, followed by an exotic, kelly-green horse wagon driven by a dark-skinned man who sat tall in the front seat. The wagon had a waistband of metal hooks from which various cooking vessels were draped—what a noise that turning wagon made as it approached the gate of our house yard. Faces peeked out. I was so bewildered. Who are these people? What do they want?

The woman held my hand more firmly as we approached the house. Drawn as I was to all her rings and bracelets, her headscarf and layers of bright skirts, I longed to dive into the tall blue grass in our front yard. It was so quiet. Where was Queen, our bulldog? It was 4:30 in the afternoon and Mother was sure to be home. We passed our sandbox and, mercifully, she appeared at the screen door; she must have seen us enter the barnyard. I was now on the front porch with my captor, facing the doorknob.

Mother asked firmly, "What do you want?" And just as the woman's grip relaxed, Mother reached out through the slight opening and pulled me inside.

"Eggs, chickens, and horses," came the ready reply.

Mother always kept a 30 dozen crate of eggs in our cloakroom. Calmly she said, "You stay there." Mother disappeared for a second and returned with the egg crate. I opened the screen door for her, and after she placed the crate on the porch floor, she turned to announce, "That's it!"

The woman hefted the gift and delivered it to the back of the colorful wagon. The driver slowly turned around our barnyard as if taking another look.

Mother watched until they re-latched the wide barnyard gate, and went directly to our crank telephone on the wall. One long ring connected 13 parties on the line. "Gypsies headed west from the Little farm," was her cryptic message.

At supper the discussion was about stealing. "They'll be back," said my father. One night a thousand laying leghorn hens were crowded into burlap bags and dragged through our southern quarter to the road. No horses were taken.

I often think of that calm Iowa afternoon that I was taken hostage. Plymouth County residents carried on but seemed to draw closer to one another.

Stampede Western Style

Two Woodward girls, two Olson girls, three Nedermeyer girls, one Hardie boy, Joe and I, were walking home from school on an otherwise dull afternoon. The boys heard that the Olsens had received a shipment of beef cattle from a ranch in Colorado and they were pasturing them in an enclosure in a field just north of our farm.

They waited until the Olsen girls were walking up their lane before convincing the rest of us to remove our jackets and wave them at those wild-eyed flared-horn critters. This started a stampede. The animals burst through our fence and beyond, onto a busy road. The event required a cowboy roundup and stretched everyone's day.

Supper was late, silent and painful. Don't forget, our schoolteacher and the roundup team were in attendance. No-good kids.

Pearl's Piano Hour

Every summer Saturday I rode the four miles to Kingsley on my bike, to a Victorian compound located on the northeast corner of First Street and Vermont. Pearl Mason, a spare spinster, was a piano teacher most village children knew as strict and humorless. Her nails would click along the ivories as she demonstrated a new piece of music. We subscribed to ETUDE magazine and were assigned research on the major composers. My two quarters were tied into the corner of a handkerchief. She took our money in her big spotless kitchen where her aged mother was usually brushing her long white hair and rocking next to a sparkling window overlooking the inner courtyard. Miss Mason's mother and I had a special relationship, which kept me coming back to run errands for her, mostly to mail packages and buy stamps. Her breath was very labored. Just walking down a short hall to a day bed was a task. Her husband, Hugh, was a big game hunter and was the subject of many photos atop the upright piano. I first tasted smoked venison at the Mason's. From April to September the piano room was a solarium. September to March, an unheated parlor; spooky in feeling as all the furniture was shrouded in white dust covers.

They were tidy folks. The kitchen floor was an enigma to me—oak planks scrubbed so often and so vigorously with homemade soap containing lye and wood ashes, it left a velvety patina the color of oatmeal. Shoes were always removed in the hall.

The son ran a large clothing store in the village, one of the anchor stores.

All of these experiences made lots of memories in my early years.

Without Music the World Would Be an Error - Nietzsche

For me, singing and dancing are life giving and are in fact lifelong. I don't recall when I didn't respond to musical rhythm. Joe and I appeared at the DeLuxe Theatre on premium night in Kingsley, during the 20's and had silver dollars placed on our heads for singing, *Bye Bye Blackbird*.

Every Sunday, the city cousins, aunts and uncles gathered at our farm for the family talent show which involved step dancing, Scottish folk tunes, piano duets by Joe and me, Dad on the violin, Mom playing ragtime tunes by ear on the piano, cousin Mary Ann singing vocal solos, Barbara Ann tap dancing in costume, group singing around the piano, finished off by my Father leading me in the waltz and fox-trot as I rode on the top of his feet throughout our house.

Miss Diller always played *Mean to Me*, on a scratchy cylinder record on the school Victrola at recess time. Grandmother had a large collection of Enrico Caruso Opera cylinders in their basement. Mighty preparation preceded the musical productions in country school and continued all throughout high school.

Joe was a serious student of the Big Band Era in the 30's and 40's and I was a very young enthusiast. He taught me the Lindy and Big Apple dance steps, which meant I knew how to dance with his friends and shared their addiction until their departure to war. The memories lingered on.

It was about this time that I aged a bit worrying about Joe—I was weighed down with secrets at fourteen.

Our hardworking parents were in bed by 9 p.m. Shortly after, Joe would come into my room and ask me to tie his tie. He was dressed to spend the evening in Remsen, four miles north of us, where there was a dance hall that featured Big Bands. He and school chum and neighbor, Billie Hardie, would shift our family Dodge into neutral and push it out on the road in readiness for the trip north. I would camp on the east windowsill of my room until the car lights were turned on and I knew they were on their way. I was unable to sleep until I heard Joe come up the back stairs to his room. It was always late but it was summertime and he was sixteen. My fun-having brother soon would go off to college and taste life changing experiences.

Rural Faith

Spring was appreciated for not only the moderated temperature but the many gifts of natural beauty, such as wild strawberry blossoms, meadowlarks warbling atop the seasoned fence posts, willow catkins, buttercups bobbing on path edges, delicate pale tiny blue flowers on green grass stems, violets, wild porcelain pink roses tracing the fence wires, all in concert with chocolate pudding dirt roads. The deep frost would ooze to the surface rut by rut and then, freeze again.

I remember one afternoon, walking home from school. Dad was at the southeast corner of our field, sitting on a high wooden box called a seeder, behind his team, Cap and Rowdy. He called to me and waved me over. In one hand he had a bouquet of velvety Sweet Williams, which he held until I settled myself next to him on the seeder. Then, he reached in his watch pocket in his bib overalls and brought out two fluffy pheasant chicks, abandoned by their mother. I wrapped them in my scarf and settled them in my lap.

As we bumped along the field, my thoughts turned serious. I asked, "How do you have faith to plant again?" The seeder on which we sat must have contained thousands of wheat seeds. I remembered last summer when our well went dry. Tankers of water were trucked 35 miles away from Sioux City, daily, to assuage the thirst of the cattle, horses, hogs, sheep, chickens, and humans.

Time can barely erase the pain of the parched livestock cries day and night. Finally, a dowsing wand dove straight down into our orchard soil. First, Mr. Justi set to digging by hand. Then, Mr. Rasmussen's well-drilling rig arrived. It looked exactly like Joe's erector set. What a racket it made. The whole neighborhood camped near my favorite Whitney Crab tree. Ten days later, and many feet deeper, the drill triggered an artesian source. Capping the water force was wild and uncertain for my family. We didn't know what to expect—but were weak from celebrating. Ice cold water beneath our orchard was harnessed by a windmill, which was immediately set in place by all the handy farmers in the crowd. In high winds, which were more common than not, it was Joe's job to throw himself at the lever on the side of the windmill and shut the turning blade down, sometimes in the middle of the night.

While I was conjuring up those memories of last summer, Dad was humming and pondering too. "Betsy, every planting season, I make a pact with God," he offered. I immediately thought about that blizzard of large hailstones that pulverized our acre of tender soybean plants so completely—only bare ground remained. Corn leaves were slivered with razor blade precision, just before they tasseled out. The rape crop was chewed up by hail and ruined. Wheat, oats and barley knocked flat unable to be recovered for threshing. Drought curled vegetation inside out and grasshoppers finished off what was left. I held my little pheasant chicks close to my cheek and looked up at Dad, who seemed so strong and invincible to me. He was still holding my bouquet in his tan hands with the rein.

The Divine Mystery

Peepers, frogs, tadpoles, baby chicks, robins, birds carrying twigs, building nests, rise of dawn, songs, mosquitoes, no-see-ums, weeds, seedlings, rain, grass growing, green lacy green, the kind of green that starts with a mist, a fog deepens, imperceptibly into a heavier lacy cathedral above all of us, green, now a chartreuse, the color of the cordial, the sharp poison green everywhere, chlorophyll captured green. How can so many green buds, then shoots, be born on each stem? Have you ever seen the way these wee green folds are packed? Man cannot do anything this complex. UPS could learn a lot from this packing design. Is this where origami masters received their training? The whole leaf is in the shoot.

Probability

The word probability gives one lots to hope for...it's a mood—a promise of probable instead of improbable. Woe unto them who wallow in the hopelessness of improbability—who enable it to succeed, who weigh down friends and children with endless reasons for doom.

The very sound of probability—a word that gives me a rush—is a feeling of a breakthrough—a change, something to look forward to—a formula for making an idea happen. It may not be clear as to where you are going, but it's certain that you're creating a climate for a new something—a conditioning for positive action. The stage is being set for expectation—life—vibrancy to depend upon...

It's like Christmas, your first fireworks, getting a driver's license and college graduation all at once to just consider the boundless wonder of probability. It's borderless— without shape. It's as high, wide and deep as your imagination can gallop—it's the tonic you should invite into your life. The very stuff that makes the difference in saying Yes or No to this cosmic thing called existence.

Dam Time and Tornado Spouts

Joe and I felt water-sport-deprived due to the summer droughts, geography and rural culture, but one summer Dad decided to anticipate the annual water shortage by excavating a 50 x 40-yard hole in the second pasture. He filled it with water from a huge shiny silver tanker from Sioux City to see if the liner could hold it. We called it a dam filled with dam water.

The cattle drank as needed. In the stock yard there was a manageable round metal tank, 4 feet across, just the right size for maneuvering around the dam, me inside and Joe's kicking motion the power. I felt like a bowsprit gliding to and fro in our forbidden vessel. Our glee did not escape the two men making fence nearby. When I shifted to the back edge of the tank to talk with Joe, the tank did a complete flip, trapping me inside, attaching my airless tank to the liner bottom. Joe tried to lift the rim but couldn't. Mercifully, the hired men could. They scooped me up shook me by my feet, laid me on the grassy bank and pounded the dam water out of me while Joe continued to swim about and push the tank toward the edge. The men tugged and pulled the tank out.

"You two are not going to have nearly as much fun rolling this tank back up the hill to the feed lot as you did rolling it down," Ed said. To say nothing of the fun we had until the imbalance act. On the way home, the clouds above were churning—always noteworthy in the Midwest.

Our bare feet were bedeviled by prickly thistle patches. We took turns pulling on the tank rim to guide it through the rough terrain. The ominous sky determined our speed. The feed lot was in sight but, thankfully, Dad wasn't. Now the ground was smoother and the tank would roll about 15 feet with each hefty push. Suddenly the sky turned navy blue directly over our house. We were motivated to reach our safe cave quickly, but first we put the tank back exactly where we found it. Next, we raced to the house and found Mother reading, unaware of the eerie stillness outside. She followed us to the cave and just as we set the heavy lid down we saw the cyclone spout touch down in the middle of our orchard. We witnessed our Greening and Whitney Crab trees being uprooted and tossed about like corks.

  Nature was tearing up our orchard and maybe our house but, as we sat on the cold damp cave steps in the darkness, we heard little and knew less. Probably half an hour later we peeked out upon a totally tranquil scene, recently violated by violent elements.

Memorial Day in Kingsley, Iowa

Memorial Day was always honored with solemn respect for our military history, starting with a parade of Veterans gathered at the Legion Hall on Main Street. They marched to the cemetery five miles north of town where, on the highest elevation, close to the Little plot, my Father stood and recited Dr. McRae's poem, *In Flander's Field*. This World War nostalgia was punctuated by Harry Werder's clear rendition of *Taps*, echoed down in the valley by Will Creasy's version.

Later, families arrived in cars filled with peonies, iris, lilacs and many watering cans as they visited their families' respective graves. Lots of visiting took place before they headed home to platters of fried chicken and bowls of potato salad.

Summer School

From the age of five I spent summers with my Aunt Kate, a former teacher and sister of my mother's father. She and her husband, Uncle Fred, who was a pharmacist, lived in Le Mars, the county seat of Plymouth. It had 4,000 people, which was a big city to me.

Their only child, Marie, was also a teacher. My education was fun and challenging. I learned how to play *The Parade of the Wooden Soldiers* on the piano. Long stemmed dandelions were used for braiding lessons. The perky blossom ends were fashionably arranged in a halo style. A neighbor girl my age and I modeled our new accessory, daily.

Uncle Fred was an Olympic skater so, of course, roller-skating fit right into our schedule. He taught us how to put one hand behind our back, swing the other with our head down low and glide endlessly on one foot. First the right and then the left, the sidewalks were so smooth. Kingsley's were rough and full of cracks.

The pharmacy had an ice cream counter. Sky high cones were the fashion. Pastel layers of ice cream kept the buyer busy. I remember picking beautiful blue bachelor button blooms for table bouquets. Fruit was such a treat. Aunt Kate ordered grapefruit sections in cans by the case—so every breakfast that was part of our diet.

When I was seven, I learned the Books of the Bible. When I was eight, I learned all the counties of Iowa and the county seats. Multiplication tables were part of my education and lots of mental math problems. Geography was constantly reviewed during dinner.

I was in such good hands and loved my continuing education courses.

John Dillinger was captured and killed in Chicago in 1932. Big Excitement!

Palpable Summer

I can feel the heat of that Iowa summer day. The orange sky radiates and throbs. The grain is in that fragile stage; too much wind, which is uncontrollable, will flatten it. Needed rain will delay the harvest and also weight the nodding arced spines and push them down like giant footprints.

The buildings are anchored; lonely sentinels on a flat piece of ground. Dry heat—it bores into your brain, the relentless sawing and soaring of the hypnotic locusts, the temperature assaulting you in waves like a pizza oven. You can't leave, it envelopes you. The sun is hotter here than any other place in the world. There are no shadows; it's always high noon.

The Rainfall Gauge

It seems that as kids our spirits rose and fell with the Fourth of July weather report. Mighty plans started as early as Flag Day—each child planned what fireworks they would buy. My favorites were ladyfingers, sparklers and cherry bombs. Joe's were four and five inch firecrackers. We all had space for running around like fireflies in the town park, dodging noisy rockets and exploding cherry bombs and watching ashy snakes move about on the sidewalk. Six-inch silk flags, made in Japan, were waved by the children during the ceremony next to the cannon. Good clothes were worn because it was a big holiday in town, accompanied by an "all you can eat" potluck picnic. Some years it rained and disappointment reigned.

Another Fourth, I remember that the phone rang just as Mother was pulling the screen door behind her—the rest of us were in the car, holding bowls of potato salad, platters of deviled eggs and bags of firecrackers. "Your cows have gone through the fence and are in my corn," barked Mr. Sheeler, our neighbor on the southern quarter. The hired men and girls were off for the holiday. Off came the party clothes; on went the fence-mending wardrobe. Dad gathered up a roll of fencing, a pocket full of staples and hammers. Joe and I were the cow-chasers, aided by Mother's gentle car guidance.

Four hours later, we tried to get the hoopla back in our front yard. That day had dawned dry, bright and perfect except for curious cows.

Wood Stove Cuisine

Betsy Stahl, a neighbor, and my mother were the closest farm wife team you could imagine. They were like well-oiled gears moving together and eager to meet a challenge.

Their food preparation was prodigious. I loved to watch but could never keep up. Little by little, they factored me into their schedule on the busiest days.

The first lesson was dressing chickens; preparing them for frying. I managed eight by 6 a.m. to their combined fourteen. Then, keeping the woodstove fed and at the right temperature - 80 degrees in our summer kitchen (sometimes outside and inside).

Betsy had two 18" black skillets and we had two - referred to as black spiders. After shaking a dozen chicken pieces in a paper bag full of seasoned flour, I started the first platter of fried chicken to be served to the eighteen hay men for dinner. Homemade sergeant-white lard and hand churned butter melted in the skillet. Keeping my distance from the heat with a long handled fork, I was in charge of the browning process.

A peck of our own potatoes was peeled for cooking and mashing, carrots scrubbed and sliced, peas separated from their pods, beans snapped, cabbage slawed, tomatoes sliced, sugar bowls, salt and pepper shakers filled, relishes, jams and jellies emptied into Great Grandmother Miller's cut glass bowls and dishes. Bread cut and plattered, lemons squeezed for lemonade, tea bags steeped for iced tea. With the first round of chicken on a platter in the warming oven, I was ready to start the second serving of chicken.

Dessert was a big deal and the men had their choice of chocolate cake, apple pie, raisin cream pie and lemon meringue, and chocolate cream pies. Sometimes they ate two pieces. Their treats were made during the cool hours of early morning. The minute we heard the men's voices in our house yard, platters, bowls and condiments were moved onto our dining room table and nestled among the eighteen place settings. All conversation stopped. Only the chicken frying could be heard. I started making gravy in the first skillet.

Dad would stop at our icehouse before coming in and bring a good chunk and the ice pick for our pitcher of lemonade and iced tea. I was busy filling glasses and refilling all the vegetable bowls for the first serving. It wasn't long before the second platter of chicken disappeared. Conversation started slowly, mostly about the quality of the hay, a light or heavy crop and where the crew was going next and, of course, the all - important weather topic.

During the meal preparations, the ballet performed around the wood stove was totally choreographed. Whatever the men didn't finish, we did, and then we talked about when the threshers would be coming and for how many days. The hired girls kept the laundry going and cleaned the house. The dishes were mostly mine. I liked learning time and motion studies from my mother and Betsy. They could accomplish some awesome tasks.

Porches

Porches! I grew up with three on our farmhouse. My favorite was the north front porch with a swing on the west side shaded by a mulberry tree. Storytellers entertained while we shelled peas, snapped beans and hulled strawberries in season. Conversations with Mother seemed to flow easier there, as if the rhythm of the foot glide softened subjects. Traffic was always of interest to country folks, a familiar horn greeting. Tunnels of dust trailed vehicles and settled in our front parlor it seemed. Sometimes our chickens strayed into the road. If their timing was flawed it meant dinner or supper for us.

The west porch was used by salesmen, company and the gypsy lady when she traded me for thirty dozen eggs.

The east porch was screened and frequented by hobo workers to whom Mother served a full meal in exchange for chores like splitting wood for the kitchen range.

Then there was Arlene Van Buskirk's grandmother's porch swing on a prominent Kingsley landmark. As we monitored village movement we sang all the songs on the Hit Parade, a popular radio show. Gregg Shorthand enabled me to capture lyrics swiftly, a skill that served me in High School reading assignments and later on in college lectures.

Grandmother Little enjoyed watching the daily activity unfold from her glassed-in front porch. There, I brushed her fine locks and listened to more early memories. In her backyard, which reached back to a hollyhock lined alley there was a grape arbor. Behind that were currant bushes and her chopping block—all very productive. In the arbor was a swing, one that one day held my son Joseph Scott Moffett in Gram's lap.

That same afternoon, Dr. Joseph Sharp, the town dentist, made a house call. He traded seats with me, extracted Gram's aching molar, and was soon on his way home. Stoic stuff!

Kitchen Kilter

It was a large room as I recall it. Four doors let you out or in to hundreds of days filled with grief, joy, noise, silence, aromas, darkness and light; the rhythm of my natal home, my family.

Two floor-to-ceiling double sash windows on the south side spread so much light through large expanses of glass. A silver hand mirror was propped up on the top of the bottom window near the southwest corner. Sometimes the light would strike the beveled mirror edge just right and prisms of color would dance on the linoleum floor under the Magee wood stove, the nerve center of comfort with its nickel bumper. The Session clock resting on its very level shelf responded faithfully to Dad's weekly turkey-feather-dipped-in-kerosene oiling treatment. Underneath the clock was a table, which housed a dictionary, a globe, an atlas and a radio.

The west wall contained a double hung window, which reached ceiling to floor. A dense woodbine formed a western porch wall, which shielded the supper diners from piercing sunsets and summer heat. Farther along, a doorway equipped with a gingerbread framed screen door in the summer with its memorable slam sound effect; a heavy solid oak raised panel door in the winter. Gypsies came to that door, as well as hobos who followed a blazed trail from town, my story-telling Grandfather Miller, neighbors, chicken thieves, the Watkins salesman and the Fuller Brush salesman.

To the right of the west door, high up on the wall was a vertical oak rectangular box, housing our crank telephone. Thirteen families were joined by that umbilical cord. One long ring was for everyone. Twelve good men could be alerted for the next day's work with one call. Neighborly help always seemed to be there for emergencies, transportation, grief, and advice. A bench bearing the scars of generations of use rested on the north wall under a big map. Wainscotting traced the wall in between doorways. The latter doorway opened into the dining room where the parlor heater was located.

    The kitchen floor was paved with foot-square black and white alternating linoleum squares. After each Saturday's scrubbing, Joe and I were turned loose with the request to wax and buff it. Running in the house was discouraged but waived during this highlighted Olympic event. The round oak table was removed to the dining room. With large soft cloths, we dipped into the Butcher's Wax can and worked a huge dollop of naphtha smelling wax into the fabric by wringing it tightly over and over. Then we divided the room in half; making sure every square received a coat as we crawled slowly on our hands and knees forward and backward. Meeting in the middle of the room, we waited for the film to setup. A pile of clean gunnysacks rested against the cloak room door on the east. We each crawled over and into one and grabbed the excess around our waists, plus any extra for padding. With a mighty leap, our hobbled bodies landed back on the redolent wax coating. We thrashed around covering as much surface as we could, polishing as we went. Reaching different doorways, we would rebound our energies and like a cannon shot, arc once more into the center, sprawling like horizontal windmills until we had reached every dull square.

    The grand finale amounted to shedding the burlap, mid-room. Donning socks, lining up in the dining room doorway and racing full tilt to pounce on the burlap heap and see if we could sail across the newly greased expanse together. Once, I caught my cheek on the sharp corner of the coal tin next to the stove but the fun far outweighed the pain of the wound.

In the northeast corner of the kitchen hung Dad's wide, supple, burnt sugar-hued razor strop under a shelf of his shaving supplies. There was also a small metal time-out stool there. I was sent there once or twice. Father's energy lingered there.

About one foot farther east, through the door to the cellar, there were sparkling Mason jars full of December to June food. On the north wall stood our Servel Refrigerator powered by a kerosene flame. High on the wall was always a Swift and Co. Packing Plant calendar featuring scantily clad models by an artist named Petti. Dad was a faithful client of Swift. His hogs and cattle usually brought the highest prices, which were announced on the noon radio news from Sioux City, after they left our farm in trucks. Dinner was often spent hushed during the stock report, followed by Plan B discussion.

The door to the cloakroom flanked the calendar. Above the door was the gun rack. As a child, I always remembered a gold wedding ring that hung on one of the supports. Whose, I never knew.

The summer gas stove appointed the east wall. A little farther was the door to a sizable walk-in pantry. Bins under the south wall counter held one hundred pounds of sugar. Cornmeal was milled from our corn at Heacock Mill, in Kingsley. Brown sugar, cocoa, salt and spices had to be purchased. Besides ingredients, the pantry contained shelves for every day dishes and cupboards of pots and pans, nests of mixing bowls and the much used rolling pin.

Canning Time

It was July and the orchard was full of mature fruit. Peaches, pears, Duchess and Early Transparent apples. Lugs of cling-free peaches and apricots also waited in the pantry. The wood stove was fired up and the sterilizer contained 12 mason jars steaming over boiling water. I removed the jars and lids and placed them on linen towels atop the round oak table. Twelve more jars went into the bath. Betsy Stahl, Mother's steadfast work partner, had already processed the apples for sauce. Peaches were plunged into a very hot water for just enough time to loosen the skin. I helped with this step. Apricots were made into jam; pears were cooked down to butter. Peaches were halved and processed. Soon four dozen mason jars were sterilized and filled with beauty that you associate with State Fairs. Food preservation products lasted throughout the winter on the four sturdy shelves in the basement. Canned pheasant, lots of pickles, tomato sauce completed the output. A barrel of Greenings, Wealthys and Whitney crab apples was popular with everyone throughout the winter.

Mother broke her own rule about ever putting anything—let alone empty glass jars—on the top basement step. She needed something downstairs for supper and quickly sent the jars crashing down to the bottom step on which she lost her footing and landed full force on her right kneecap which was soon imbedded with shards and glass chunks. I ran to the doorway and noted the royal mess below. Mother seemed pinned-down by a quickly-forming red pool. Her disgust and pluck pulled her up but failed to let her walk.

It was Dad's busiest time in the barn but I knew that I had to get him and get to him quick. Would he know what to do? I didn't. He ran ahead of me, inching down the glittery steps. He ripped Mother's apron and with several two-inch strips he wrapped a tourniquet above her knee. I watched from the landing and felt sick looking at her blood-soaked leg. She was so calm. Dad picked her up and moved swiftly up the stairs to the outside hand pump, which I managed to prime fast as Dad stuck Mother's leg under it quite awhile as he picked off the glass. I could tell by her wincing that it hurt, and besides the water was ice cold. I ripped up old linen towels to redress the wound.

This had been a tender moment for me to observe my parents silently giving and taking in a moment of stress; tacitly caring for and about each other, which impressed their child greatly.

Midwest Gold

Our farm in Garfield Township, in the northeast corner of Plymouth County, was a pilot for Hybrid Seed Companies. Corn was king and more bushels to the acre was the game. Bright yellow and kelly-green labels of DeKalb, Pioneer and Pfister signs labeled our 8- to 10-foot examples for the public to monitor if they were interested.

Dad also planted and harvested three cash crops; namely soybeans, rape (canola oil) and hemp.

Henry Wallace, FDR's Secretary of Agriculture visited our farm in the 30's for the purpose of introducing his program of slaughtering baby pigs in an attempt to control pork prices in the market. My father was not impressed.

One July Day

On July 15, 1934, Varney Speed Liner inaugurated Continental Air Lines with a 503-mile route from Pueblo to El Paso, Texas, with a stop in Las Vegas.

That same day, a major updraft of wind struck great-grandfather Henri deLambert's stock barn north of Pierson—lifted the sizable roof, corner to corner and set it down in a nearby pasture "as smooth as pie" as Mother, his special grandchild, put it. I was ten years old and part of the crowd that gathered about.

The whole hay mow, filled with the first cut of hay was exposed and neighbors and strangers appeared to gawk, then in time reappeared with huge expanses of coverings, tents, even the canvas used to catch the bales on the hay binder.

Grandpa had a huge number of animals to feed and keeping the hay dry was the unifying worry. Women sacrificed their oilcloth tablecloths and heavy quilts. The next day the hay was protected. The next day, another turbulence arrived and lifted the errant roof, corner to corner settling it intact on the corner posts as if directed.

This all happened in God fearing country and I watched those farmers accept the last meteorological miracle as stoically and quickly as the first.

Summer in Iowa was always erratic and unsettled. Hail, tornadoes, drought, daytime darkness, churning wind clouds. Your gaze always turned heavenward in an attempt to anticipate the beginning, middle and end of each day.

Custom Butter

My job, every Saturday from eight years of age onward, was to churn good rich milk into butter. After a certain number of cranking turns liquid turned into solid chunks which multiplied into a single lump. Then I drained off the liquid, or buttermilk, and poured two glasses for Dad and Joe, an expected midday treat.

I made sweet butter, which I later learned was the preferred baguette accompaniment in France.

Mother took over at this point introducing salt and yellow food coloring, mixing diligently until it resembled the pounds at the village store. The best part was watching the big finish as she worked it into the low crock, twisting her Grandmother's grooved paddle to and fro over the crest of the butter mound creating a design, not unlike her pie crust art. She had a style. Next week, the Daisy Churn was filled again.

Passion Payoff

Mother was an undefeated woman's basketball captain in High School and, in general, a serious sports fan and competitor. She and Dad played Tournament Golf and Bridge. Her goal was always self-improvement.

Joe and I spent many hot summer afternoons playing Hearts, Gin Rummy, Canasta, shades drawn, a fan oscillating, lemonade cooled down with ice from our own ice house. A baseball game was always on the radio announced by Dutch Reagan, to whom she was devoted. She made more noise than Joe and I together when the scores were tight.

Then, every fall, the *Des Moines Register and Tribune* had a Big Ten Football Contest. She loved contests and entered, predicting every Big Ten Football score, accurately. The prize: a Shaeffer Pen and Pencil Set awarded to her by her hero—Ronald Reagan, in Des Moines.

My July Parlor

    I was watching the hard-boiled egg of an Iowa sun stare at our side house yard. Watching, watching until the big elm tree shade took over and cooled the grass under and all around the sagging clotheslines attached to distant silvery wooden poles; that expanse of grass, regular, deep green and wavy on the soles of my summer-tested feet.

    I think I was nine; old enough to carry out my Mother's suggestions. I remember I disliked being told to do something that I was just about to do, like gather eggs (I was terrified of our ruling rooster), bring in the clothes off the line (sometimes the rain won), or dust the front stairs (it never showed).

    I set about preparing my outside parlor. I removed the oval mirror that usually hung on a wall near our back porch and hooked it on a handy nail on the tree over the bench in my new space. First I tugged and hauled out three stained and bleached pine wash benches from the Close house, where Mother washed clothes every Monday. I leaned one bench against the generous elm tree, the other two on either side. I carried out three large white ironstone basins from our pantry one at a time and centered them on the benches. Castile soap, bars the size of half a brick, completed the wash station. Fresh Turkish towels were stacked in a seasoned clothesbasket nearby. Water—precious water, lifted hand over tender hand from the battered bucket in our cistern was emptied into all manner of assembled containers. Clean, cold water was essential.

    I fairly ran to my shady room carrying heavy full pails in each hand, sacrificing two inches of sloshed water off the top before they came to rest by the trees. Agate pitchers were filled and placed to the left of each basin. I inspected the high impact areas two times before I felt satisfied. The first team drawn load of straw pulled into our farmyard. It was Ray Olsen, the stacker. He was a much sought after artisan for he could stack loose straw to resemble a perfect loaf of bread with just a hint of a crown and make it stay stacked; a performance of skill.

The crew of grain shockers soon livened up the yard. I had lifted the edge of one of the many towels in the basket and tipped it over the edge so the men would know to use them. I sat in the lilac bush shade 20 yards away so I could watch the men use my parlor. Three or four sat on the lawn nearby awaiting their 'wash up' turn. Some luxuriated in the act of lathering up at the benches. Their huge ham hands would slap the backs of their tanned necks and then they'd run up and down their leathery arms lightening quick, finishing up with their bronze faces and hairlines.

Then water would fly all over the green carpet as they'd liberally rinse. With thumb and index finger, they'd swoop up the weighty basin and arc the sweet foam away from the station. Toweling off appeared to be a gentle, deliberate massage. I quietly reappeared and picked up the saturated towel heap and hung them on the clothesline a short distance away.

The air was subdued. Even my brother and his best friend Billy had lost their zeal to tease. They'd been picking up bundles and tossing them since 7 a.m. It was surprising to watch the burliest of the labor lot comb his satin black hair and shape the waves. He appreciated the mirror. Dad was the last one. He didn't say anything but I know he must have been amazed that there was enough water and dry towels for everybody and relieved and pleased that I stayed in the background tending to business. As I hung up the last of the wet towels, I could hear through the open kitchen window the hum of twenty hungry men being fed inside. I would save the unused water to put on our two new trees in the front yard. That afternoon I went in the back way to our kitchen to see if Mother saved me my favorite piece of fried chicken and a juicy slice of apple pie before I returned to tidy up my July Parlor. Maybe I'll hang a basket of Brown-eyed-Susans off the clothesline pole next time.

Harvest time revealed the beauty and grandeur of our fields. I watched the undulating sage green oat carpet for one-quarter mile bounded by my Father's tight fences. Then, like paint-chip gradations of color the fields of wheat and barley turned from burnished gold to ecru to biscuit. Any day the neighborhood-shared threshing machine would groan, creak and lumber into our barnyard, coaxed to a halt by Mr. Roy Laude, a massive gentleman wearing his snap brim sweat-soaked straw hat, the only man who understood this metal monster. His mission this day is to reduce our quilted fields to grain and bundles over the next three days. Mr. Laude was so curious to me. Patient, always running everywhere about his machine as if a purposeful dance and tool tinkering was all the juggling needed.

Twenty more men would visit my July Parlor and eat at Mother's table. I loved this part of summer—grain threshing time.

Alfalfa and Corn

When brother Joe was eleven and I was nine we loved to play in the hay mow. The big hay hook would grab a chunk of hay and lift it to the high peak at the top of the hay barn door and slide along the metal track to the center of the mow. Joe would pull a rope and trip the load onto the mow floor. Then we would toss the mound into a deeper pile. Barefoot, we would climb up the 20' ladder on the inside barn wall into a stifling air-less space, fragrant with the aroma of strong, dry alfalfa. We tried to see how far down into the scratchy heap we could land. Dad didn't always know we were doing this. Later on, in the deep summer, he would ask us to dive into the middle of all the hay in the mow to check the temperature. If it was warm enough to cause combustion, we quickly grabbed bundles of it and tossed it for hours diffusing the heat. We felt very useful doing this.

Our diving-derring-do did not stop there. We also found other adventures in the corn bin. Since we raised acres of corn, it was imperative that all the corn be fed into our corn sheller, mobilized by Tony our mule, who was trained to walk in circles from the beginning of the wagon load to the end, filling another wagon with hard kernels; some would be planted next year, the rest fed to our livestock. We waited until the hired man and Dad spent two days filling the corn bin, because diving required lots of corn for our adventure. We climbed up the outside bin ladder and squeezed through the chute hole at the top and dropped down. The corn enveloped us just like sand. We kicked hard to find the floor.

Suddenly there was a bang. Ed had positioned the corn chute in the hole at the top. Nobody knew where we were. We each hit for the bin sides as that blast of maize shot down and pinned Joe to his 2x4. I was barely hanging on with cramped knuckles on the other side, but fell into the slippery crop and was swirling in the growing pile. We couldn't yell out because we were off limits. Now it was up to my waist. I tried to scoop it away from Joe but I couldn't reach him. On the corn came, pelting my head with sharp marble points, abrading my arms.

Then—miracle of miracles, chest high in a prickly sea of corn, feeling sick with heat, the machine stopped—the end of the load. Joe and I looked at each other and whispered "We've got to get out of here, but how?"

"Let me scoop it away from me first and I'll work around you and push it to the other side," Joe said.

We thought of Dad and of the hired man listening to the grain still in motion and wondered if that could be. Luckily, animals had to be fed and we neatly escaped through the window of the treacherous corn bin. Supper was very welcome and a relief.

Switchel for the Shockers

Acres and acres of barley, oats and wheat were assaulted by Roy Laude's binder in the mid-summer. Teams of men rode out into our fields in hayracks pulled by horses. Pitching bundles into the hayracks was hot; itchy, sweaty work. Often competition would take over and quick work was made of the chore.

My job was to locate the block of ice beneath the sawdust in the ice house and chip enough to keep the switchel cooled down in the big crock of ginger, sugar, water and vinegar that we fit into my red wagon. It was Mother's version of ginger ale and it went down pretty well with the parched men. Gingersnap cookies accompanied the treat. Maneuvering four wheels over the field ruts slowed me down but when the men saw me coming they met me, which cut down on spills and ice melt. The pleasure they took from this refreshment was gratifying and made me feel so useful on the return trip.

Iowa Fall

It was six on a November morning. Raw, slant sleet weather. Dad harnessed Rocky and Blaze, our black Belgian team. I could hear their bridle jangle when they threw their huge heads up and dropped them down, in tandem, outside the house yard gate. Mother was finishing my midmorning snack of homemade bread, sweet butter and bread and butter pickles. She then bundled me up in my snowsuit, cinched my hood really tight. I watched her slip into weatherproof canvas overalls. Then she led me down the sidewalk to the horse and wagon. Dad was already on the high seat holding the reins. We climbed up beside him. Only four years old, I loved being snug between my parents. We traveled a half-mile down the gravel road and entered an open gate into our cornfield, where sage green, bamboo-like, tall, dry sentinel's leaves clattered in the wind. The corn stocks were loaded with heavy foot long ears.

Dad's command stopped the team at the outside row, as Mother settled me in a safe spot at the end of the wagon under the seat so I wouldn't get tagged by maize missiles. Now both parents were ready to husk corn, a picker on each side of the wagon set up a rhythm as they snapped the stems and hurled the ears, building up a cargo that tumbled all around me. Once, I peered out from my perch and got banged on the head but no real harm. Time for my snack. Mother kept cheering Father on as she matched him ear for ear. They were a good team. The row was picked clean. Tomorrow the next row, until the field was finished. Today's load was delivered to our corncrib, later to be shelled and placed in our corn bin for animal feed.

Special Gifts

Words were like special gifts handed to me.

I remember…the day dad explained 'finite' to me.

Mrs. Seimens, my History teacher, filling a whole blackboard to illustrate 'drawing inferences' to me.

Mrs. Quirk dismissing an idea as 'preposterous'.

Grandmother Little noting the meaning of 'affinity'.

Malady—another word for sickness, in the crossword puzzle.

I kept a journal of new discoveries and appealing phrases throughout my school years. It became a part of our farm auction.

I remember a comic strip Dad and I enjoyed together, *Major Hoople*, a buffoon who deemed his words so important that in winter they froze and hung in the air.

Snowbound

1936 was memorable; especially the winter. It started snowing all over Plymouth County in early November and we couldn't get it stopped until March 1937. Wild blizzard conditions prevailed at 30 degrees below zero.

There were riveting moments for the whole household. Dad, the two hired men, Ed and Reifel, and brother Joe dug a 100-yard tunnel through the snow from our house yard porch straight across to the big barn and two feed lots to gain access to our milk cows and many white face beef steers, Hampshire Hogs, sheep and horses. Ice had to be chopped in the water trough daily. Feed in the barn had to be distributed; stalls cleaned and freshened. The force of the wild wind managed to drive oat straws into the weathered rump hides of the steers, housed in an open shed off the big barn. We were all daunted by the porcupine imagery.

The wind would shift drifty snow and create artistic curls and razor sharp crests. Eventually, enough design collected against the barn, all the way up to the haymow door—a story and a half high. Joe and I snaked through the tunnel with our skis and slid out the haymow door, landing on our house porch, dead ahead.

The Boarders were active weather watchers when they weren't tunneling and caring for our animals. Two hired girls, Emma and Audrey shuffled "to-do" lists. Miss Diller home-schooled Joe and me whenever possible. Mother and Father sprawled playfully as they giggled and tied an unfinished double-bed-sized quilt, spread out on the parlor floor.

Bread was baked daily, always an aromatic and culinary treat. The kitchen was fully engaged because our cellar inventory contained last summers' orchard harvest and garden provender. Pheasant meat was canned. Side meat and ham were smoked. Chickens were close by; another tunnel project. The pantry bins contained 100 pounds of flour and 100 pounds of sugar so baking continued in our toasty Magee stove. The kitchen pump functioned after vigorous priming. Wood chunks stacked and buried on the back porch fueled the parlor stove except when we burned ear-corn which created a kaleidoscope of brilliant color behind the parlor stove's mica windows; magic to a twelve year old girl.

We were isolated. Everyone in our school district was, except for our crank phone on the kitchen wall. The phone was only used for dire emergencies, like when a horse fell headfirst down a well in a neighbor's grove, or when hay-men, hay stackers, or grain shockers were needed. One long ring rallied labor when the sunshine and crops cooperated. Rain was a bittersweet event, if ill-timed, during haying season.

Perpetuating Santa Claus

My father loved to tease. His specialty was the Santa Claus myth. Our Christmas Eve custom was to attend the Evening Services at the Kingsley Congregational Church. So many of our family friends and their children were members there.

The church sanctuary was redolent of balsam fir. A two-story high tree, loaded with handmade ornaments, popcorn and cranberry swags, wrapped labeled gifts filled the branches next to the Altar. All the children occupied the first two rows of seats at the edge of the Altar. High expectations controlled our excited thoughts.

We heard the church doors open, some stomping and muffled harness bell sounds, interspersed with lots of movement and then, a deep-voiced "Ho! Ho! Ho!" burst forth into the sanctuary. It was Santa Claus!

We all stood, turned and peered down the aisle as Santa waved to us. He talked about the difficulty in finding us because there was so much snow. He greeted Bob Moritz at his aisle seat, then Santa moved toward the tree to start the gift distribution. We were tense. Lillian's name was on the first box. She bounded out of her seat straight for Santa. "How's your sister, Dorothy?" he asked. Santa always knew so much about our families. His shiny leather boots matched his wide black belt. The white fur trim on his jacket and his beard were rich and thick. Wide white gauntlet cuffs attached to his white gloves reached to his elbows.

George, Billy, Joe, LaVern, Audrey and Elmer rose as their names were called. He was mingling with the recipients now and inquiring about their siblings and parents. As he continued to search through the branches for more gifts he removed his left glove and then his right.

"And here's something for Bette." As I leapt up to receive my treasure I saw the Masonic ring on which Dad would strike his kitchen matches. I wailed, "Daad!" and went stone silent. I was pretty upset. My friends were clearly bewildered by my outcry. My seven-year belief in Dad's Santa fun was shattered. Soon parents began to gather and bundle up their children for the trip back to their homes.

Joe never said a word as we returned home to open up the family gifts under our own tree. I secretly think that he was sad that my world of make-believe was over, too. Dad and Mother watched the road, a tunnel bordered by eight-foot snow walls. Upon arrival home we settled around the central heater in the parlor to open our gifts which changed the subject to humor and appreciation. Mother disappeared into the kitchen to prepare her traditional Oyster Stew, which we ate in silence at the kitchen table. Buttery seasonal stew accompanied by toasted homemade croutons.

This particular Christmas Eve, I was mindful of the many discussions Dad and I had over the years about just what Santa would like for a midnight snack before he delivered our special gifts for Christmas morning. He discouraged my annual suggestion of milk and cookies, and would allude instead to Santa's weakness for fresh oysters. And so, for years, a pint of fresh oysters was the offering. He always left an appreciative thank you note and a reminder to be sure and check out the porch rooftop for sleigh and hoof tracks, which I always did and they were always there.

We all drifted off to bed. The house was very quiet and I mentally assembled all the Santa clues and marveled at Dad's magical stagings to keep the myth alive. Next morning, Joe and I found a science set and a bicycle for our big Santa gifts. I made peace with being wise and more mature but I do recall the impact of innocence leaving my world.

The History of Kingsley, Iowa

Brothers William and Fred Close from England came to Iowa in late 1876 to tour the area with intentions of purchasing land for investment. They purchased 3,000 acres at $3.50 per acre to divide into quarter sections and construct basic farmsteads to be rented out to small farmers. After seeing a good return on their investment they were joined by their brother James. The Closes eventually purchased 16,080 acres and townships in Plymouth County at $2.40 per acre.

On September 18th, 1880 James and Fred platted the village of Quorn on their farm in the southeastern part of Plymouth County. The name Quorn came from a favorite fox-hunting place in Leicestershire, England.

By 1882, it was a bustling frontier town of 300-400 people with several businesses, a school, a post office and a newspaper. The railroad was building its way westward and it was hoped and expected that it would pass through Quorn on its way to Sioux City and points west. However, it was built as far as the present site of Kingsley, and even one quarter of a mile farther, when construction suddenly came to an end and a station was established where Kingsley now stands.

All went well with "The Maple River Railroad" until they came up against the Close Brothers at Quorn. John Insley Blair, the railroad builder, had faith that Quorn could not survive without the railroad. On June 22nd, 1883 he purchased land within one mile of Quorn - the land that presently comprises much of the town of Kingsley, the deed filed in the county recorder office in Book 'O', page 19. The cost for the purchase of this land was $1,000.00.

Blair hired Nahum P. Kingsley, a native of Rutland, Vermont, to lay out the new town. Many of the streets were named after those in his hometown and state: Park, Vermont, Burlington, Barre, Rutland, Dover, Brandon and Clarendon, as opposed to those of Quorn: Britain Street; Main, Elkhorn, First, Second, and Third Streets. Close houses appeared throughout Iowa. Easily identifiable white two-story clapboard houses. Ours was used as our wash house and woodbin.

The village of Quorn was carried in the Plymouth County book into the 1920's. The old Kingsley Mill first stood on the banks of Rock Creek. It operated there during the 1870's and consisted of two French millstones called buhrs and machinery necessary for the processing and cleaning of grain. Owners, the Heacock Brothers, visited Quorn and noting that it was a prosperous area, decided to move the mill across the prairie to Quorn. The dam and mill were constructed during the fall and winter of 1881 and resumed operation in April 1882. The mill not only ground corn and wheat into feed for livestock and food for local farmers but also produced flour and products for sale to people far and wide. In 1910 the name was changed to Kingsley Milling Company.

Presently, the French grinding stones can be found at the northeast corner of the Kingsley City Park as a memorial to the mill's existence. By 1890, Kingsley's population was 649, with about 60 businesses. A newspaper article from 1899 read, "...about 80 businesses and professional men are doing a flourishing business in Kingsley." In 1901, a telephone franchise was approved with Hunter Brothers of Sioux City, and changed to Kingsley Telephone Company, several years later.

The Kingsley Bank, later Oltmann & Phelps, then Kingsley State Bank, withstood the Bank Holiday of the 30's and is one of the only three charter members of the business community still open.

Mr. Blackston

There was no certain summer month on our 100-acre farm—that glacial deposit of rich loam, sixteen feet deep—and no day without worry that a piece of machinery might shatter in the field.

Someone, usually Dad, but it could have been our hired-man Ed Meister, would ride Rowdy at a three gait rate into the house yard, clutching two shiny pieces of a disc, a corner of a plow share or a jagged metal shard from the corn planter that needed a blacksmith's touch. Mr. Blackston, the farmer's friend, was located four miles away in Kingsley, which meant that Mother was once again the chief courier. Her endless care-taking tasks would always cede to field emergencies. Off she would tear due west over the ruler-straight corduroy gravel road in our Dodge sedan.

Reflecting on these essential errands years later, I wonder what those Blacksmith visits were like for a woman. Was my mother the only female to enter that double-garage sized shop on Main Street, where the sun barely pushed in 6 feet at the entrance ramp and farmers and perhaps daily visitors were seated patiently in the Rembrandt black shadows? I remember glancing furtively at that crowd when I passed at noontime during my high school years. Was my Mother intimidated? Was she taken care of right off? Repairs were serious business and time meant something.

On summer nights, as the supper hour approached, Grandmother Little and I would visit on her front porch facing the

Burlington Street sidewalk in Kingsley. You could set your watch at 5:45 p.m., when Mr. Blackston would trudge homeward up the hill, his right hand clamped on the handle of his dented metallic gray lunch pail, his head down as if burrowing into a stiff wind. To me he seemed like an apparition clothed in blue-black greased fabric with skin to match. His step had the weight of his anvil and his form resembled a fist of muscle. His appearance never changed. I wonder now, what was his private life like? Did he use Lava Soap? Did he ever get clean and wear a white shirt on the Fourth of July? Did he go downtown on Saturday night like everyone else did? How did he get so blackened every day, anyway?

I never heard it mentioned at any time, but suspect that Mr. Blackston's problem solving skills were quietly invaluable, single-handedly holding together the rural farming community east of Kingsley (and probably south and north) in the 30s and 40s and beyond.

Here's to you, Mr. Charles Blackston! You were famous but we hardly knew you!

Lisle Style

When I was a High School Sophomore, Principal Gill called me into his office where he spoke glowingly of Leadership. Two-thread nylon stockings were very popular with the female students but most impractical and expensive. As a special favor, Mother gave me permission to wear hers that day after making sure that I could handle them without snagging any part of the nylon. Mr. Gill was a good friend of my family. I felt trapped as he offered me 25¢ to buy a pair of lisle stockings at Eddie Blaisdale's downtown store to model the rest of the school year.

Skipping school was fun; not so, my mission. Mr. Blaisdale said, "Something for your grandmother?" Limply, I answered, "No, me."

"Are you in a play?' he asked.

"Sort of," I muttered and left.

After school, Ardis Karlson and I sat on Grandmother's front steps, tugging at hunks of stocking and stabbing them with sharp pencils. The right leg was holier than the left I laundered the battered lisle briskly after supper.

The next morning they were almost dry when I put them back on, sagging nicely around the frayed holes. I stopped in Principal Gill's office after General Assembly and hoped to convince him that lisle just wasn't able to compete with the active life of a teenager. He sadly agreed.

The Tightwads Four

I always loved to be with elders when I was young. They knew stories that seemed magical to me. Magical because they endured so many hardships—so much loss with so little bitterness. That impressed me. Farming was a good family life but hard, steady, dangerous and demanding work.

Grandmother and Grandfather Little followed the pattern of their peers. In the early 1900's after they had raised their children, they moved to Kingsley and made a new life; not an easy adjustment because their chores disappeared and the men were lost. Grandfather walked four miles to our farm, daily, just to bring my Mother an apple. A train trip to Chicago was planned to visit their daughter, Helen. Grandfather had a tooth extracted shortly before. Infection set in and took his life, ending his brief retirement.

Inactivity drained the dreams of many farm husbands. The women had never known retirement so their schedules were comprised of necessities and pleasure, which led to a steady and vibrant community life. Playing Bridge was their vice. They called themselves "The Tightwads".

Four widows took their turn, weekly, serving supper and a table of bridge afterwards. A dozen of eggs from our farm was the usual prize. More stories and old-fashioned menus were such a treat. My schedule was carefully built around theirs. Again, they forgot about my ears when I cleared the dining room table. I was everyone's granddaughter and they were my special friends. They were my prudent mentors and my yardstick for behavior. Disapproval was enough.

The Fabulous Fofts

There was a brick building on Main Street, in Kingsley, that had FOFT in custard yellow blocky letters nestled in a centered rectangle on top. Cars were sold to tempted buyers inside the double doors below. Gale Foft, my father's age and a good friend, was memorable to a small child. I never remember him wearing anything but a 3-piece suit, quite unusual in a rural area but he was a car salesman. Cars were status symbols and Gale knew how to improve your stature. Besides his easy manner and expansive laugh, he sported a canary diamond pinkie ring—another first, which he was happy to tell me about.

Gale was married to a lively lady named Eulala who suffered near fatal burns in a kitchen fire in March's Café. The Friolator sputtered onto her face, neck and arms. Her scars were always artfully draped with streamers of chiffon, long before designers created gossamer stoles. She was different and of great interest to me. Her large, unfurnished Victorian home had newspapers for wallpaper and dark woodwork throughout. When I was a High School freshman she asked me to tea. No one had ever done that before. From the enthusiastic greeting at the front door to the final goodbye, panache ruled.

We talked of lofty things, few I recognized, but the grand piano in the parlor commanded great attention. Upon the silk fringed shawl rested ornate silver frames featuring her three daughters, all graduates of The Pasadena Playhouse in California. Shirley, leaning against an airplane, was an Aviator; Llewelyn, a Betty Grable wannabe, posed accordingly; Gwendolyn stood with Agnes DeMille, the choreographer. They were the closest connection to Hollywood our town knew. I was so star-struck, the movies being the big escape. There is life after Kingsley, I decided that very afternoon.

Historic Thursdays

It was Thursday afternoon after high school. The Quilters were moving sharp steel needles, seven stitches to the inch through a snowy white field, yards long and wide. I would always find my Mother, Grandmother and their good friends in the church parlor, around the big rectangular quilting frame built by Gus Swanberg.

They called it Thursday Circle; I called it a treat.

Mrs. Ripley's lace cookies, Gram's ginger cream cookies and Mother's dream bars were accompanied by lemonade or milk. As usual, I was invisible as they resumed their stories, visiting while their worn hands moved above and below the quilt, smoothing, sending the needles up and down, keeping the pattern taut. Individual names were embroidered all around the edges where they sat.

A young bride was the highest bidder at the church auction. She gathered it up in an unwieldy lump, trying to see the names on each side. Finally, she found a table surface on which to spread it out flat. There on that expanse so much was represented.

Stitches, yes, but oh, the heartache, joy, and despair in those heroic stories.

Elephant Excitement

An 18-wheeler was idling in front of Grothaus' Café, and no less than fourteen people had gathered on Main Street in Kingsley. They stared up at the Hollywood sized paintings of lions on one side behind licorice black bars that looked like they were made of iron instead of black paint. Above the animals' heads was RINGLING BROS. hand lettered in gold and outlined in red. The other side of the trailer featured a mammoth pachyderm frozen in a trumpeting gesture, sending the longed-for high screech into the rural village. The circus is here! The circus is here!

School kids poured downhill at lunchtime and smelled the circus wagon as they pummeled each other for position. They knew all the steps. After lunch some would cut school and go directly to the field beyond the City Park. There they might even hold a rope for the roustabout as the men unravel the innards of the tent wagon. Or fill endless buckets of water for the animals, or help unfold the Big Tent on the ground, or sort out the trunk of stakes needed, or just watch the circus mahout work with one of the elephants and pull the right rope on silent command.

She Was the Berries

Life is just a bowl of cherries! Now that is close to what my Grandmother Little said when she was pleased. Isn't that the berries? Whatever does that mean? How did the values of perfection get assigned to berries? What is the origin of these phrases that get shuffled along over decades of reunions? It has a sense of approval and well being and brings lovely comfort to me in a wave of nostalgia recalling Gram's aproned figure, arms akimbo in celebration. What did the berries signify in her life—a life too far from some of her daughters—a dry well, taxes, poor crops and still, for me, praise.

Daily Words

Coffee as thick as molasses would be boiling on the wood stove in her dark kitchen corner. By 6 a.m., Grandma Little was in her wooden rocker on the glassed-in porch facing the well-traveled sidewalk one half-block from the Kingsley High School. The paperboy faithfully placed her tri-folded *Sioux City Journal* inside her door at 5:45 a.m. On collection day she would always provide him with a plate of ginger cream cookies.

The headlines were scanned, then quickly buried under the page containing the crossword puzzle. Fifteen minutes was her completion time, generally. The dictionary was rarely consulted.

Local Color

Winnie Price

Every graduating Kingsley High School Senior had to arrange for a photo session with Winnie Price, village photographer for the yearbook and social documenter. Repugnant developer chemicals could always be whiffed on the street near her studio. Her fat black and white cat lounged among the latest photos propped in the big window in front of the expanse of black curtain.

There would be rare sightings of Winnie outside of her premises. From hat to boot tips she was a specter in black, marinated in chemicals wafting along like wind gusts. Who was she? Where was she from? Family? Mentors? Camera education?

Charlie Cunningham

Charlie was always dressed as if he were going to catch the train to Chicago. Maybe he did. He lived in a room near the train station, walked with the aid of a smart looking black lacquered stick, topped with a silver ornament. An impressive gold watch chain always accompanied his tweed vest. He would speak either with a brogue or an impediment. Who was he? Where did he come from? What did he do? Family?

As a child, local color was just part of your life experience. The answers to my questions were always, "We don't know why people decide to live where they do."

All small towns had boarding houses. Kingsley had three, which contributed greatly to intrigue. A stranger in town kept porch dwellers, telephones and kids on bikes very busy.

A Sunday Drive

Sunday afternoon drives around our farm section were rituals during my young summers. Granted, the reward was ice cream at the Pierson Drugstore, six miles south. I definitely outgrew this family outing during High School, but an offer from a classmate was another matter. That meant exploring new territory, privately, with a date.

This Sunday afternoon, Ross Reinking pulled into our yard in a 1940 model Oldsmobile 4-door sedan. The cream-colored finish looked as if it had been ladled on with a spatula and then seriously buffed. Wire wheels and sage green trim and cream leather interior completed the picture. It didn't matter that he was unannounced; any company on the farm was exciting. I was out of the house before he came to a stop.

"Try to find the horn," Ross grinned. I peeked in his driver window, looked left and right for a button on the dashboard, but failed. "It's this metal ring inside the steering wheel" he said, pleased with his secret.

"Wow!" I stammered.

"Wanna go for a ride?"

"I'll say!" and I jumped in beside him.

"Where shall we go?" Ross shouted across the very wide front seat.

"Let's pick up Billy and Helen. They're in Grand Meadow, 18 miles east of us," I offered. We did and they were so excited about Ross' new car. Then we decided to go to Kingsley, 30 miles away and see if Margaret and Miles could go for a ride with us. Three in the front and three in the back, Ross approached a major intersection of gravel roads with signs warning "Danger—Soft Shoulder" posted on both sides.

As we're rolling through the intersection, Ross turned and said, "Here, you drive, it's lots of fun," and passed under me while he still had one hand on the steering wheel.

"I've never driven a car," I sputtered. "Where's the brake? I can't learn so fast; what if I get the gas pedal mixed up?"

"You can't," said Ross, who'd driven a tractor since he was twelve years old.

I still have my foot on the gas and the back seat passengers pound on me to turn right toward Remsen. I do. There is silence, absolute silence as six teenagers roll peacefully over once, then twice, till we reach the bottom of the ravine.

We'd landed on the right side of the car. Ross turned off the ignition. We all noiselessly, slowly, numbly crawled out of the left windows front and back and staggered up to the road's edge and sat like birds on a wire, staring at nothing, for what seemed like years. We were in shock.

Finally, Ross put his arm on my shoulder and said, "I'm going to walk into town and get a wrecker." I nodded sickly and thought, the wrecker is coming on a costly Sunday to dig out a new family car that Ross' parents haven't even seen. The car dealer delivered their new beauty yesterday. I can't imagine what his parents, returning home from vacation, will say. Still, no one spoke. I was shaking. The experience just hung in the air. I can never tell my parents; my brother; yes, I have to tell someone. How will I find enough money to cover the expenses? Money? I don't have that kind of money. I started to shake again and heave; Billy and Helen were starting to talk.

Hours later, Ross and the wrecker showed up, driven by a

friendly man who extolled the strength of the Oldsmobile chassis. He stood on the road next to Margaret and Miles, sized up his mission, and then unreeled a very long chain from his sturdy wrecker. He literally swam down the gravel ravine to hook onto the flashy chrome bumper resting below. He came back up, set his wrecker wheels with blocks, started up the power and began to right the car. We're all staring at this slow motion recovery while he double checks the chain speed.

"She's really heavy," he yelled. "$5.00 and you can keep on driving."

We all stepped cautiously around what could have been our tomb. The driver's side had a few scratches on the fender, but that rolled landing was good to the hearty cream enamel.

"I know a body man," the helpful driver said. "You were lucky kids."

Yes, weren't we? Conversation was spasmodic; fright-laced with *Wow!* and grateful expressions that Ross had the $5.00. He was a hard working farm boy who insisted that the accident and repair were his responsibility. I was just sick about the whole thing. Ross delivered all of his passengers to their homes and then the family car to his.

It was an afternoon ride on a Sunday with friends, on an otherwise perfect day in July 1939. As far as I know, no one ever shared this experience with anyone. I didn't learn to drive until I was thirty.

Wool into Wisdom

Minimally educated, frugal farmers, my Grandmother and Grandfather Little were determined that their seven children and grandchildren, including my brother and me would be educated. Their seven daughters attended college – no small feat on the family budget. Their two sons served in World War I.

When Joe and I were six and four, our grandparents gave us twenty-one sheep, expressly to provide for our formal education. The summer Joe was ten and I was eight our chores amounted to herding the flock into the house yard to mow the grass. They cropped the grass very close when contained in our snow fence pens, which meant we had to move the enclosure about four times a day and never let any animals escape. The history of sheep herding, we learned, is one-go-all-go and that was trouble. They would immediately head for Mother's flowers, shrubs and young trees, and quickly devour them. It was a two-person job herding this amorphous flock. Returning them to the barn every evening, getting them fed and watered, took forever.

The summer season would be uncomfortably warm for ewes to carry around a heavy layer of wool so we arranged for Mr. Sheeler to come to our farm on a specific day and shear our sheep. He was a master wrangler of all manner of disposition and I marveled at his strength and speed. Nary a nick of the flesh did he inflict. As wool piled up, Joe and I would card and stuff it into burlap bags, ready for the next step. We had to arrange for the sale, shopping for the best price per pound in the *Sioux*

City Journal. Dad would haul our added-value product to market and bring back our check, which went immediately into our bank account.

We owned our own ram, a cantankerous creature to be avoided in the open pasture or close quarters in the barn.

Spring presented another chore: midwifery. We became pretty handy at saving baby lambs in the birthing process. Mothers didn't always bond with their offspring so the mudroom of our kitchen served as a nursery. Ketchup bottles equipped with nipples were filled with cow's milk and fed to the ravenous orphans. Feeding time was before and after school. It was a great day when they joined the rest of their family for food and gamboling about. Then it was time to cull the flock, arrange for sales, either to neighbors or the livestock market. Dad and the hired man helped us decide what breeding stock was best for the next cycle.

Our grandparents taught us a lot about responsibility and earning to learn. Joe entered Pre-Med at the University of Iowa, and I chose Business Administration with a minor in Fine Arts at the same school. $1,500 was the cost of each semester.

Politics 101

When I was in High School, I spent a great deal of time with Grandmother Little, whose home was two doors away. Farm chores were a part of Joe's early mornings and late afternoons and so he was allowed a car when he was a freshman. I stayed with Grandmother and loved it. She was my political tutor. She had unusual radar for a farm widow, fixed on F.D. Roosevelt and the Democratic Party. I learned about his C.C.C. and WPA Programs. Commentator Raymond Graham Swing satisfied her international and domestic news curiosity, daily. Crossword puzzles and long letters to and from her seven children kept language arts alive. I could never share this enlightenment with her son, my father, mother, or their siblings' families, who were Republicans; a Midwestern malady. My excitement flagged on the weekends spent on the farm but was revived in my eighth grade Civics classroom. I was impressed with Gram's interest in educating me and she seemed pleased, too. It was our family secret. How did she escape the Midwestern Puritanical Passion? She was a news junkie, and an avid follower of the political columnists who addressed domestic and international news in the daily *Sioux City Journal* and sometimes the *Des Moines Register and Tribune*. All my family used our library, which was located on the third floor of the Kingsley Opera House. The books were arranged on the green felt of two regulation slate-bottomed pool tables. I was the book borrower for everyone. Radio was also a constant in Gram's day; only tuned to the news.

I remember seeing "America First" pamphlets on her library table in the front parlor in 1939. Aunt Helen, who married a Chicago lawyer, brought them on her last visit. Gram was not amused nor interested in this Isolationist Movement which attracted Nazi sympathizers, but my Uncle Walter and Charles Lindbergh, our American aviator hero, were. I can recall Gram's ire when Neville Chamberlain, Prime Minister of England, appeased Adolph Hitler. We talked and talked every evening. It's no surprise that Political Science taught by Professor Jack Johnson at the University of Iowa was major in my curriculum. He knew how to engage a curious student. I considered changing my Business Education major, but didn't. I just became a political student for life.

Little did I realize when I married Hugh 0. Moffett, the National Affairs Editor of LIFE magazine, on December 22, 1951, that I would be privileged to attend the Democratic National Convention, and see history made first hand. I talked to John Kennedy before he took his seat on the *Meet the Press* panel with Morrie Spivak, in Washington D.C.'s Mayflower Hotel Studio. Then, Hugh beckoned me in the hallway to witness Kennedy joining Lyndon Baines Johnson's Texas Headquarters to initiate their run together, an unbelievable coupling to my mind at the time, but true history. I later attended Kennedy's Inaugural Address, accompanied by a very pregnant Helen Rowan, whose husband, Roy, was also an editor for LIFE. The day was brisk and very windy in January. Extra-cautious police insisted that Helen and I view the proceedings from a specially constructed platform placed directly across from the speaker's podium, should Helen need to be separated from the crushing crowd in a hurry.

As the morning progressed, Robert Frost appeared, his silver hair tossed recklessly by the constant wind. Kennedy, hatless and handsome, awaited his commissioned poem, *The Gift Outright*, which blew away as the podium caught fire. More history witnessed up close and personal. Order was restored and Robert Frost continued reciting.

Serious snow started falling in Washington DC the day of the Kennedy Inaugural Ball. Traffic circulation was impacted throughout the city; a foreign element invaded without warning. The Inaugural Ball's glitterati soon wrestled with private, then public transportation issues. Hugh and Roy solved ours by buying a milk delivery truck off the street, complete with driver. The high wheel clearance negotiated the rivers of filthy slush running curb to curb. My flesh-tone silk satin pumps dyed to match my strapless gown were spared saturation as Hugh carried me from the hotel to our commandeered chariot. It was approaching Cinderella's coach story because we had a real curfew. Helen and I were dry and fancy while our husbands led on, damply. Looking about, colored puddles from custom-dyed shoes created a unique floor palette at the ball entrance.

Upon entering, all eyes were refocused on the Royal Box as Jackie arrived, looking stunning in a flesh silk satin shift with a delicate overlay of thousands of hand sewn beads, both translucent and the bugle type. What a dazzling entrance! Jack, in his tuxedo, just beamed. Music from the orchestra brought them to the dance floor. Shortly everyone joined in. I thought of Grandmother Little, who would have been daunted by how my life was unfolding after all those tutorials around the wood stove years ago.

On November 22, 1963, we had invited forty people to be our dinner guests at our home in Port Washington, New York. Hugh had recently been offered the International Affairs Bureau for LIFE, and we would soon be leaving to live in Paris, France, for five years. I was intensely involved in food preparation when the phone rang. A sobbing friend asked if I had heard the news. I hadn't, and just slowly delaminated, thinking—could there be such hatred in our county? Hugh was instrumental in getting the story for LIFE and stayed with the details for ten days. The TV was on constantly at home. As Joe and Mark, our young sons, and I were going out the door to Sunday school, we witnessed Jack Ruby killing Lee Oswald. So much violence was numbing.

Scattered Shards

One Monday, in the late fall of 1943, I was in my sophomore world at the University of Iowa, in Iowa City. I was full of confidence, still celebrating my Dolphin Queen reign, solidifying friendships, enjoying most of my courses (especially Professor Jack Johnson's Political Science and Professor Johansson's Creative Writing classes) when my world turned upside down.

After my ten o'clock, I collected my mail as usual at Currier Hall, a large dormitory for women. I ran up to my room to open the thick envelope from home and slowly and curiously unfolded a pale yellow page, entitled AUCTION NOTICE in bold black letters. Under that, J.B. LITTLE FARM AUCTION, CONTENTS OF THE HOUSE...I couldn't go any farther. Contents of my birthplace, my brother's, my father's and his six siblings. Contents of my house. I was sobbing, I felt empty, orphaned and betrayed.

Does it mean when you go to college, you lose your home? Your roots? What did this mean? I couldn't dredge up one hint in Mother's letters since my return to school— nor was anything mentioned during vacation. I stared and stared at the yellow page. Maybe I misread it. I realized that I had no way of preparing for such a piece of news.

Lunchtime passed. Suddenly, it was Gym Class time. I just couldn't reconnect with reality. It was sometime before I unfolded Mother's letter, which started, "Dad and I sold the contents of all our buildings, in addition to the house. The land and buildings were sold at auction to a bachelor who people say is a good farmer. Preparing the inventory was a big job, we found out. Betsy, my dear friend and hardworking neighbor helped me. Her husband, Ed, was very useful organizing Dad's tools. Dad was busy estimating the amount of hay in the big barn loft and the hundreds of corn bushels in the corn-shed bins. Small grain in the barn bins had to be measured, too."

Nostalgic images are popping up now. The Close House. I sank down on my bed. This 1800 English clapboard building was also a part of my birthplace. When you are born into a setting, there's deep comfort that accompanies that, a security that can never be shattered by change, I thought. There on the wall was the sepia photo of my father sitting in the very seat that I occupied in the Garfield No.5 one-room schoolhouse. The copper boiler occupying a high shelf every day except Monday, when it was placed on the small wood stove and filled with buckets of soft cistern water taken from just outside the breezeway, a cement apron where we cracked hickory and black walnuts after school for a snack and fudge that Mother made for Sunday evenings, sometimes. The wash machine where Mother rescued me from going through the ringer with a bed sheet.

This flood of loss consumed hours. Then I was seized with the need to talk to Mother and Dad. We had a phone in our room but long distance was rare and expensive. I placed the call and Dad answered. I started to cry and choked out my heartbreak, which I could sense, was theirs, too. He started, 'The new owner has rented the farm to a family, so, of course they would use the entire house. Mother and I talked about putting your childhood items in storage. I'm sorry about your Northwing, Betsy. We knew you'd be disappointed but we just couldn't find the right arrangement. We had a lot of decisions to make."

Now, I didn't hear any more words. My head was swirling with

Northwing inventory images: my doll's porcelain tea set; my doll's aluminum cooking pots and utensils; cigar boxes full of paper dolls and their Betty-designed wardrobes; my French doll from Grandmother deLambert with a bisque face, real hair, a white kid leather body and handmade leather slippers. The Dione Quintuplet paper dolls from Canada and their extensive wardrobes; Sally, my Horseman doll from Gram Little; journals I kept about books I had read; first editions of N.C. Wyeth illustrated books; *The Bobsy Twins*, *Uncle Remus*, a beautifully illustrated *Aesop's Fables* volume, my dictionary, which contained the words "finite" and "inference". My brown Bakelite radio (we were one of the few electrified farms)—so important because it brought the world of popular music to me, the Big Bands from famous nightclubs, Meadowbrook and Glen Miller, all the way from Glen Island Casino late at night, personally, to me under the covers of my bed. My lifeline. All of Joe's precious John Deere miniature metal machine toys still lay buried in the sandbox where we'd last played "farm".

I recovered and managed, "How did the auction go?"

"It went better than we expected."

"It was popular with antique dealers," Mother added. "Four generations of Little Inventory really brought them out," Dad interjected.

"Now what?" I asked.

"We want to build a new home near Lake Okoboji." I knew they never wanted to be farmers, but were obligated to manage the farm for Gram, so now, finally, they could plan their reward. Mother came back on the line with tears that blended with mine and let me know that they have been drowning in memories but must move on; an example that has served me well. I grew up a little that day.

Independence

The Chicago Northwestern Train was huffing on the tracks next to the Kingsley train station. My parents helped me with my heavy luggage as I boarded to take my young adult leave of home. I was going to Chicago to earn a living. Mother and I found things to say but Dad was pretty silent. He followed me up to the steps and to my seat, then pressed $200 in my hand and said, "This is the last, Betsy." We hugged so hard we surprised each other and then he turned. I saw him again waving from the platform. I was so happy, so scared, so free, so independent, and so young. I think that gift was a secret between Dad and me.

People cannot deal with too much wonder all the time. Experience counts and adds up to a lot of pleasure, discomfort, sadness, good times and love. Sometimes the reaches of the spirit are just deep seated, but the only way to make sense of the journey is through the stories. I find that I returned home without having left and learned that when you grow up you take your childhood with you. Leaving home is your education.

Earning and Learning

When I left the University of Iowa, in 1945, I followed my college roommate to Chicago and shared an apartment with her. She loved her new job with the Blue Network, which later became the ABC Network, located in the Merchandise Mart on the Chicago River. I was interested in the world of fashion so I started with an unannounced visit to Bonwit Tellers on Michigan Avenue. Personnel was located on the 9th floor, and a secretary sat behind a desk, ready to direct you. I asked to meet the personnel manager and was suddenly in the office of Jack Brown. "What do you want to do?" I was ready with, "I would like to become a Designer Sportswear Buyer."

"How old are you?"

"Nineteen."

He disappeared into his office, typed furiously for minutes, it seemed, ripped out the pages and presented me with a two page letter of introduction to a Miss Marguerite Edwards, "who was just hired from us by Marshall Fields at the highest salary ever paid a woman in merchandising. Go straight to her department on the third floor. She's excellent and tough." True and welcome words.

I wanted to learn and was willing to do whatever it took to earn Miss Edwards' acceptance. Others were less eager to seek her guidance, I learned later. I entered the floor slowly, observing all the displays and interaction on the part of staff and customers. A short woman stood to the side dressed completely in black, even her canted stovepipe hat added to her severity. "That must be Miss Edwards," I thought, all the while trying to buy time as a customer. My early buoyant courage gave out and suddenly I was breathing her air. "I'm here to see Miss Edwards."

"What about?" she barked. The last of my energy blurted, "I have a letter from Jack Brown."

"Come in," she said. We went through a door that looked like part of a secret wall. There was no place to sit. Merchandise, papers, bills, tickets, hangers were piled up everywhere, from the floor up, everywhere. She finished reading the letter and said, "Put your things over there," pointing to an open desk drawer. "We're going to the thirteenth floor. You will work up there taking stock counts, posting unit control data and checking every piece of designer stock that comes into the Department for three weeks."

The employees on the floor watched with sympathetic interest as I received my instructions. I was working for tough Miss Edwards and marveled at my opportunity. Humorlessly and firmly she talked about workmanship. In college, I'd made my own formals, and the experience prepared me to evaluate workmanship. Missed stitches, raw seams and uneven hemming were rejected and returned to the manufacturer after garments were turned inside out. Miss Edwards threatened to deduct the wholesale price of each designer product irregularity from my paycheck if the merchandise reached the sales floor.

Popular designers, such as Clare Potter, Tina Lieser, and Clare McCardell, were very important in the 40s, and were modeled widely in society. Some designs for bathing suits needed instructions for proper presentation. I remember returning from lunch one day after delivering three strappy black jersey bathing suits to the display department in the morning. Securing the State Street window of Fields was the goal of every department. Each suit was presented, but backwards. Two hours later, the window was closed and the mannequins re-draped.

As far as I know, Miss Edwards missed that rare display. She seldom went out for lunch or formed friendships in the store; she was a loner who concentrated on budget, business and developing new market contacts. Her success was not surprising. She rented a five-room apartment in an elegant brownstone on Lake Michigan. Miss Edwards thought nothing of planning our next season's budget at her apartment five nights straight. I was grudgingly permitted to call my roommate. My interest in my job was eclipsing my life and I became puzzled by Miss Edwards' "take over" attitude without benefit of explanation regarding the monopolizing of my time. We worked on papers spread about on a bed. There was no furniture in the apartment, no food in the refrigerator. A doorman was the conveyor of food that she ordered each night. Jack Brown was right—she was tough and a good teacher. I wonder how well he knew her. Did anyone know her?

One night she abruptly announced, "We're going to Louisville, Kentucky, tomorrow."

"What about our department? We can't both be absent."

"I have told the store," she said. That amazed me. I barely slept on the extra sheet-less bed with trunks forming odd obstacles all around me. The lake lapping nearby was audible through the open French windows.

We were going to Louisville to visit her family and she especially wanted me to meet her granddaughter, Shirley. The next morning the doorman called. We got ready for the trip. I was still wearing department clothing selected for the week. We caught the train and settled into the parlor car. I watched the real estate melt away and Miss Edwards dozed for quite awhile. I had little money in my wallet. She had the ticket. I tried to rouse her for dinner but she slept on. When we neared our destination neither the conductor nor I could wake her. He said, "I'll wire ahead for a wheelchair." I was concerned and realized that I knew nothing about this woman, less about her health. She was not responding. Thank goodness the conductor was also concerned. I knew she was tired—all she did was work—but she never slept through workdays. What was causing this slumber?

And her family—oh dear! I glimpsed the Louisville Station sign out the window and a row of stoics standing on the platform underneath it. They resembled a primitive painting. Was this somber group her family? A young platinum-haired girl stood alone. Was that Shirley?

Miss Edwards was dead. The conductor carried her off the train and placed her in the station wheelchair. I leaned in the doorway and seemed to be as silent as the strangers. No questions; just quizzical stares. Shirley offered that Miss Edwards didn't take care of herself or her diabetes. This was a real revelation and the cause of death. Shirley said the family owned a pharmacy. I thanked her for helping me understand what happened. The return ticket was located in Miss Edward's purse—I stayed on chatting and sharing all the pertinent information of my life with Miss Edwards with Shirley until train time.

I bid goodbye to Louisville and felt sick as I endured an orphaning—a deep loss of my mentor. It was all too short a tutelage. Now what? I called my roommate upon my arrival and she shared my shocking news. Then I called the store. My Merchandise Manager offered me the job of Designer Sportswear Buyer and asked for my Fall Sportswear Budget. I had the final copy, which he approved. It was on Miss Edward's desk waiting for action. I went to New York and spent it just as we had discussed. It was always a gamble. Did I buy the right merchandise? What a guessing game. I had beginner's luck.

I brought little change to the Sales Floor. The average age of the force was 71. They were a very competitive colony of Rumanian Jewish ladies who gave 100% of their attention to my requests and their clients. In all, they kept the department figures in the black. Miss Edwards knew their worth and I was unseasoned but grateful.

Full Circle

In 1959, I lived in Port Washington, New York, and Joe was in the service in Stuttgart, Germany. He called me and suggested that we visit our folks as the family we once were. Our folks moved from the farm and built a new home in Iowa. I was now caring for four children and was urged by my husband Hugh to definitely go. Joe and I met in Arnolds Park, Iowa, located in the lake region of the state, and we settled in for a good visit. Only childhood memories of summer connected us to this area. We discussed our itinerary, which veered closer to our birthplace on the farm. Dad said, "If you go to Kingsley, be sure and notice the assisted living facility at the edge of the park." He sent me to a corner located at Brandon Street and Park Street. I have lived on Park Street in Brandon, Vermont, since 1968. What a prophetic direction that was! I did visit the care center and learned that the Director, Mrs. Kuhn, had a daughter who lived in Brandon, Vermont.

Joe and I drove slowly through our old hometown, trying to place our past. Finally, we went into Marsh's Café and sat in our old booth, just watching people come and go. Every once in awhile, I'd note a hint of a family resemblance. A woman, as curious as we were, approached, asking,

"Aren't you John Little's children?" We left the conversation there. We explained our mission and then headed for the farm, full of expectations.

It's so weird, how the four miles east of Kingsley had changed. Farmers had removed their fences and farmed right up to the road, taking full advantage of that productive soil. I wondered about erosion. The car turned in through the barnyard gate; a camper was parked by the house yard gate. We sat quietly, looking at our (and our father's) birthplace after all these years of building memories. Could this really be where our convoluted journeys began? The sandbox was still there.

A scholarly bachelor bought our farm at auction and filled our house with books. He emerged, asking, "Is there anything I can do for you?" We waved and said together, "Noooo!" and left the yard, painfully unfulfilled. Joe drove slowly to the section corner, walled in by eight- to nine-foot tall cornstalks. This dangerous density had not changed. We remember accidents caused by the game of chicken there. The gravel crackled and crunched beneath our slow moving tires as if it, too, was staring and crushed by what it saw. Neither of us spoke—looking back, my bedroom windows blankly returned the stare. We didn't mention anything to each other about the section of sidewalk with our handprints, but I remembered. We certainly weren't prepared for this moment and attempted to console one another by saying, "Well, we have moved on."

We drove to our one-room school, Garfield No. 5, on an acre of unplowed land, which is now someone's home. On to Pierson, my Mother's birthplace, and the charming brick home of Great Grandmother Lina and Henri DeLambert. Only the foundation remained next to their herb garden paths.

Before we returned to our folk's home, we decided to drive slowly through Kingsley once again. We approached the eastern-most property, once owned by Miss Pearl Mason, our piano teacher, who charged all of 50¢ an hour-for her strict tutoring. The wrought iron fence still enclosed a perfect Victorian compound, located at First and Vermont Streets, marked by white letters on deep navy enamel signs. The next street was Rutland Street and Second Street followed by Dorset Street and Third Street. Burlington Street and Fourth Street was Grandmother Little's address, and lastly, Brandon Street and Park Street formed the western-most boundary.

Intrigued by street signs that neither of us recalled, we asked Mrs. Kuhn who advised us to review the platte at the Oltmann and Phelps Bank. It seems that during the celebration of their Diamond Jubilee, Kingsley appointed the streets, officially. People from Rutland, Vermont settled Kingsley. As they pushed west, they could be traced by their tradition of using their name. In Rutland, Vermont there exists Kingsley Street, Kingsley Avenue, Kingsley Arms, Kingsley Commons, and many families bearing the name of Kingsley. This was unexpected information for Joe and me after all these years.

Headed due North, we turned our back on so many school highlights but we'll always have our memories. You can go back but I wouldn't.

Our folks dreaded our disappointments but filled our visit with moments that mattered.

Smooth Take Off

Shortly after I took over the Designer Sportswear Department at Marshall Fields, I had the opportunity to work with manufacturers on personal design. I envisioned a shirt with a diagonal zipper closing and a breast pocket on the left. Since I loved textiles, pure fiber such as wool, rayon, cotton and silk, plus variations within that selection were used.

Another buyer, Barbara Cappeau also had Wednesday afternoons free. I went horseback riding, usually. She took flying lessons at the airport.

After Cappy won her wings, she insisted that I accompany her as co-pilot. We flew an Eurcoupe, which is smaller than a Cessna with totally simple controls. I was quite impressed.

I heard pilot talk around the hangar about Ceiling and Visibility Unlimited and thought the acronym CAVU would be a good name for my shirt.

Labels were made and affixed to the prototype. After a discussion with the manufacturer about the cost of the garment, averaging-in the cost of all fabrics and sizes involved, my merchandise manager approved the order which would be delivered to all employees for the storewide promotion that was coming within two weeks. That was a big step but my biggest idea was to convince Cappy to get her Flight Instructor's approval to lend us the Eurcoupe for the Celebration of my CAVU shirt.

Undaunted, he said he was looking for an idea to promote flying lessons.

"Where's this plane going?" he asked.

"Into my department at Fields via our huge freight elevator," I responded.

Still too reasonable to be believed, he said, "I've got to go to Chicago and measure the entrance of the elevator. You reserve the time and guarantee the insurance."

When I approached Marshall Field, he seemed very seduced by the publicity for his store and permission was granted.

The great day dawned and all the CAVU clad personnel were in their respective departments. Quite a crowd found their way to the 3rd floor, including LIFE Magazine Photographer Wallace Kirkland, who was assigned to cover the story by his boss—my future husband—Hugh Moffett, then the Chicago Bureau Chief for TIME Inc. Kirkland, a 6'4" man with a brush cut, known simply as Kirk, accosted me and demanded, "Who's the boss here?"

"Mr. Fields," I stammered.

"Get him on the phone." I did, nervously asking if he could please come down to my department because this photographer was insisting that I get up into the airplane.

"Give them what they want!" He screamed into the phone. "LIFE MAGAZINE, WOW!"

I introduced him to Kirk, hoping that he would get into the plane. He turned and coaxed, "Let's both get in." I was a wreck because we couldn't step on the wings as the skin was so fragile and I noted that we didn't want to damage it.

While we were discussing the dilemma, Kirk had produced a two-story ladder, a one-story floor fan and a 48-inch silk white scarf. Mr. Fields was the beaming pilot and I, the co-pilot, looking for all the world like Amelia Earhart, silk scarf streaming behind my long auburn hair.

Kirk shot at least forty rolls then departed to develop them at his Michigan Avenue office. "I shall return with some prints for you," he shouted. The store simmered down finally, but the city did pay attention and kept the stories going.

When Kirk returned, he mentioned that his boss had recognized me. "I know her," Hugh had said. "That's Betty Lou Little from Kingsley, Iowa—as editor for the *Des Moines Register and Tribune*, I was asked to be a judge for the annual University of Iowa Dolphin Queen Contest held on Homecoming weekend, and I chose her." Kirk was still amazed. "Well, she's working at Field's now," Kirk had informed him.

Kirk suggested we have lunch but I demurred.

"No, I don't think so," I said.

"I'll take you to the Executive Dining Room," he offered.

"You're on," I rallied—thinking it would be fun to invade the old boy territory. Another coincidence was revealed during lunch.

"Do you remember when WOI (World Office of Information) came to the University of Iowa?" Kirk queried.

"I do. You wanted co-eds to pass out packages of Coffee Tones, a cigarette substitute, as Lucky Strike Green had gone to war to keep the soldiers happy," I recalled.

"My photos were picked up by *Pathé News*," Kirk noted.

"And my parents were not too pleased when they saw the story on *Pathé News* reel in the Kingsley Iowa Deluxe Theatre," I remembered.

I thanked Kirk for his generous coverage of my CAVU promotion and we parted—but not before he insisted that I meet his boss. I did, and the magic carpet ride took off.

SCHOOL

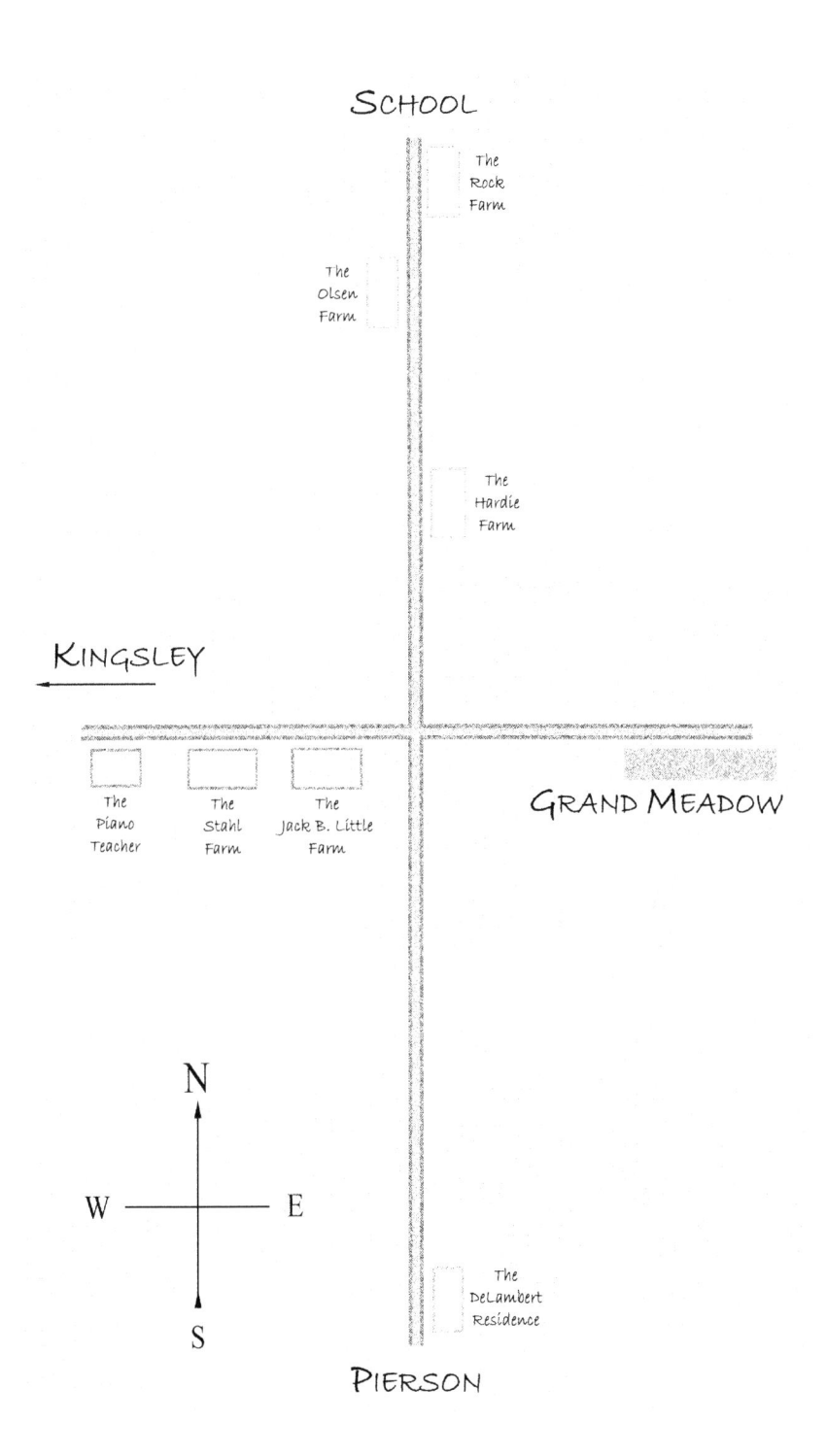

The Rock Farm

The Olsen Farm

The Hardie Farm

← KINGSLEY

The Piano Teacher

The Stahl Farm

The Jack B. Little Farm

GRAND MEADOW

N
W E
S

The DeLambert Residence

PIERSON

Acknowledgements

I would like to express my gratitude to Molly Kennedy, who typed the manuscript; Caleb Kenna, who read the first draft; Beth Miller, who prompted the map, and Mark Moffett, who provided the cover.